CW00661484

Dedication

I dedicate this book to the people of Wednesfield, past, present and future.

To Ivy & Don.

Best wishes

Ray Fellows

10-9-10.

Wednesfield Our Village

Ray Fellows

Malthouse Press

Copyright. Ray Fellows. 2009
Published 2009
ISBN 978-1-907364-00-6
Printed by Lightning Source UK Ltd

To contact Ray with your memories

Telephone (01902) 739592

Email fellows-raymond@yahoo.co.uk

Published and produced by
Malthouse Press
Grange Cottage, Malthouse Lane
Barlaston, Staffordshire. ST12 9AQ
TEL (01872) 372067, Timcockin@yahoo.com
(specialists in competitively-priced print-on demand books)

Contents

Illustrations

Introduction

Some of the photographs that have been used to illustrate "WEDNESFIELD OUR VILLAGE", were given or lent by individuals from all over Wednesfield.

Many of the photographs show the village as it appeared from the turn of the last century, up to the 1960s, how the High Street has changed with redevelopment can clearly be seen.

Some of the stories have been passed on by some of the Wednesfield's older generation. Some of the facts and figures have been acquired from Wednesfield Library, extracts from Wednesfield News have been used.

I would like to congratulate those who have been down this path before, they have written excellent books about Wednesfield's past, but I hope that mine is a little bit different.

I hope that you can relate to some of the stories and events that have taken place in and around Wednesfield, or "Wedgefelt", as older readers may call it.

Please excuse me if at times it seems that I have strayed away from the subject, or jumped from the early part of the century to the 1960s.

I hope that the views that appear in this book will be helpful to those who wish to know, and understand Wednesfield better, and convince them, that its more recent past is worth recalling.

It has taken me 20 years to finish this book, please enjoy it. I believe people will understand when I refer to - *at the time of writing* - that this could have been at anytime over the last 20 years.

My thanks and appreciation go to my wife Kath for being so understanding, and also to Jim Evans, Eric Riley, Mr Webb, and Mr and Mrs Lloyd. Thank you so much. Also to Jacqueline Fellows, Ned Williams, and Tim Cockin, for their help and support. I would also like to extend my thanks to The Express & Star newspaper, and The Black Country Bugle.

Ray Fellows, Wednesfield, 2009.

1. Battle of Wednesfield

WEDNESFIELD, or as it was more commonly called Wedgefelt, occupies a prominent position in the early records of our local, and national history, the name is evidently derived from Woden, the Saxon God of battle. It was most likely to have been between A.D. 907 and 911, in the fields between New Cross, Willenhall, Portobello, and Wolverhampton, that one of the most sanguinary and decisive battles ever fought on English soil took place, resulting in the death of the Danish kings, Eowells, Halfdene, and Hinguar, several noblemen, and thousands of soldiers, the loss of their baggage and total defeat of the Danish invaders.

There are now, no traces of this battle, mining operations, the plough, and other agencies have removed or levelled the mounds that were raised over the remains of the slain. In the late 1950s a sword was found in an old well, on land commonly known as Bacchus end, your guess is as good as mine as to whether this sword was anything to do with the battle, since

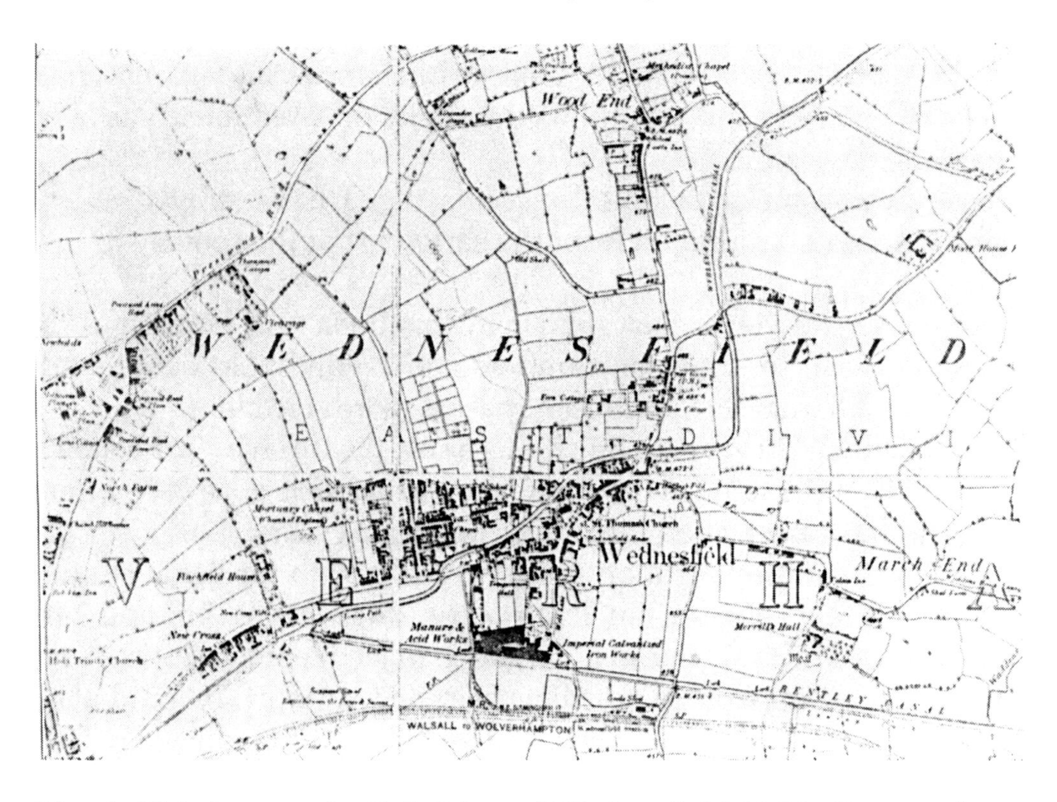

Fig. 1. This is an early O.S. Map of Wednesfield 1891. You can just pick out the supposed site of the Battle of Wednesfield at the bottom of the map, towards the left.

no one knows the whereabouts of this sword, it's most probably in some museum somewhere.

I must point out that there were three reports about the battle, the various Anglo-Saxon Chronicles give only bare details. The Laud Chronicle says 910: in this year the English army and the Danes fought at Tettenhall. The Worcester Chronicle states 909: in this year the Mercians, and West Saxons fought against the host near Tettenhall on 6th August and were victorious. Ethelward, an Anglo-Saxon chronicler, dated the battle to 909. He stated that a battle ensued, and the English without delay obtained victory at Wednesfield (near Tettenhall), and the army of the Danes was put to flight, overcome by weapons. Wednesfield has just had its 11th hundred anniversary since that battle of 909.

2. Wednesfield in the 1890s

THE POPULATION of Wednesfield in 1891, was 4,949. Wednesfield Parish was very extensive but its built-up area was very small over a hundred years ago. Like so many other villages it centred round the church, consisting of High, Charles, Rookery, Hall, New, Cross, Hickman and North Streets, with a few dozen houses at Wood End, and March End.

The Cottage Homes in Amos Lane already existed, whilst on the New Cross boundary, Wolverhampton was about to build a new workhouse, and Poor Law institution, but which is now New Cross Hospital.

There were of course quite a number of farms and cottages, but the general rural aspect was almost undisturbed. The Weldless Steel Tube company, and Mander Brothers being about the first to erect works of any size within the parish. It should be noted, immediately adjacent to the Midland Railway Station, there was the canal down Neachells lane. Wednesfield was well served even then with canals. Along which many thousands of tons of coal were transported by barges, from Holly bank, Ashmore, and collieries on Cannock Chase. A few trains per day provided the only transport for the travelling public, so unless one could cadge a lift in a road vehicle of some kind, well, one had to walk.

Generally, folks seemed to be more hardy then, and thought little of a jaunt up to "Hampton", or down to Willenhall, besides time was not such a big factor then, and the demon of speed had not taken control of the souls of men.

A little later on, a horse-drawn brake used to ply from Wednesfield to

Fig. 2. Wednesfield High Street in the early early 1900s. Swatman's Barbers, on the right, the barbers pole, sticking proudly above the doorway.

Wolverhampton, run by a chap called Tommy Moore; this eased matters somewhat.

All the same, road travelling was no luxury, for the badly sprung vehicles having iron tyred wheels, and most roads all ruts and holes - like today are you thinking! - deep in mud, or dust according to the weather, made a journey by road a jolting experience which people jokingly said was good for your liver.

Travelling conditions being what they were, and worse in earlier years, it is small wonder people tended to stay mostly at home, so they, their children, and children's children, married and raised families which became deeply rooted here, becoming the backbone of the community in trade, business, and social life' generally; though rather self-centred perhaps in their outlook on life.

You may well recall such family names as, Adey, Barnes, Beech, Birch, Clay, Collins, Davies, Davenport, Done, Evans, Foster, Green, Gregory, Griffiths, Hadley, Hyde, Lane, Lewis, Mason, Mattox, Millichamp, Pal-

Fig. 3. An early photograph of workers in the fields at Ashmore Park. Date unknown.

lant, Peers, Picking, Pritchard, Pursehouse, Rowley, Snape, Sidebotham, Stringer, Stevens, Squire, White, Williams, and many others, of whom a few of the 'old uns', could still be with us, whilst many of their descendants figure largely in our business and social life. Old Wednesfield therefore was considered not such a bad place to live in, indeed it was deemed to be healthy by comparison with neighbouring townships, and in spite of primitive, and crude sanitary conditions, and the fact that hundreds of people had one, or more pigs, fattening up in their back yards.

There was no deep sewer, but most houses had a piped water supply, whilst wells, and cisterns were numerous, bathrooms hardly existed, but that did not prevent people having baths. Yes, baths! and maybe more often than some do in today in the age of bathrooms, with hot and cold running water.

Some old buildings of that time, are now no more, and the loss of decrepit houses, and cottages are not mourned, but one or two are missed, though they had their day and served their purpose.

There was the old 'pound', which was a walled in enclosure, in which stray cattle, and horses, were impounded until claimed by their owners, by application to the police.

The pound stood near the canal, immediately opposite the Dog and Partridge, a few yards away from the public toilets.

There was that old desolate building at the top end of Hickman Street, with broken leaded lights, used one gathers as a school in the distant past, but where Mr Tom Whyman plied his trade of carpenter, joiner, undertaken, and the art of making and polishing coffins.

This business was later carried on by Tom's son-in-law, the well-known Fred Pickering and Sons. Over a hundred years ago the industries of Wednesfield were small by comparison with today. Indeed, it is doubtful if any firms employed over fifty workers, and most of them would not attain even this figure, most of the trades and crafts were native to the district.

The machinery used then was elementary, and primitive, by comparison with today. The life of the average worker has thus been almost completely changed, through new innovations, the machinist of those days, has in many cases, become merely the machine minder of today.

The skilled craftsman was of great importance, in field, and factory, and remained so for many years.

This was more marked in small towns, and villages, where new ideas, and methods, were adopted more slowly. It was common to work longer hours, fifty, sixty, and even more. Despite the greater demands made upon physical strength, the strain, and stress of industrial life then, did not appear to produce the nervous disabilities which are all too common today.

Agriculture, and farming were the main occupations, and still absorbed most of the people on the land. The large farms were held by such families as Bradburn, Brevitt, Clay, Chester, Downing, Eastwood, Hyde, Lewis, Smith, West, Williams, and Wooton.

Work was slow and laborious, being the days of the horse-drawn plough, harrow, and roller.

The old hand scythe was freely used to reap and to mow, the sower went forth sowing, striding up and down the furrows, scattering the seed by hand, with a rhythmic swing of the arm, and presenting a picture like the 'Parable of the Sower' in the New Testament.

Locks and keys were another industry in Wednesfield, although Willenhall will lay claim to being the main town producing them, Wednesfield played its part.

Willenhall was after called "Lockland". It was also known as Humpshire,

Fig. 4. The Dog and Partridge Inn is on the left. On the right the wooden building stands where the old pound once stood. This was used to impound stray cattle and horses.

the latter name had its origins in that, in the bad old days many workers within the lock industry were hump backed, this was through working long hours bent over the workbench, with no breaks for meals, there was a time when master men could apply for boys, born and reared in the workhouse, to be bound to them as apprentices, indeed some of these master men themselves had been workhouse born. Move over Oliver Twist!

Many of these apprentices were terribly underfed, and overworked by their masters, the brave ones often made raids on the pantry, at night. Disraeli makes reference to Willenhall at this period, in his book 'Sybil'.

In Wednesfield, however, more were employed in making keys than locks, the workers being known in the vernacular as "Kay Bodgers", and "Lock Bosters".

Apart from a few places that employed a number of people, most key smiths worked on their own, in a small shop, in the backyard, assisted in some cases by members of the family, wives included.

The people of today would have been amazed to have seen the decrepit treadle lathes, relics of the past even then, that were used in these backyard

Fig. 5. This photograph is said to be Ashmore Farm in the early part of the 20th Century. It could be of Neachells Farm. I was given it some years ago and told it was Ashmore Farm. Do you know?

shops, and the good, even beautiful work that was turned out on them.

Most of these small backyard shops did work for the large makers of keys and locks in the district, including Willenhall, and Wolverhampton.

They usually supplied the key blanks, and paid when the work was returned completed.

Money was often advanced on an order at the time it was issued, and it was not uncommon for such money to be spent by improvident men, in a few days, "on the beer", so that by midweek the money was gone, and no work had been done. Such mortgaged work was called "corf", a term used from the origin that is difficult to discover other than words that explain that a set to had to be made on this "corf", to finish and deliver by the weekend, in order to get another order. A sub was often required on that one in order to keep things going, at home, such lapses made things very bad for the home.

To make amends candles and lamps would burn far into the night, so that work could be completed in time. Some of those who indulged in boozing sprees were quaint characters. A clever key smith was offered a regular job at a very good wage, but refused it, with the remark, "No I cor tek it, a regular job wants a regular mon, and I bay one", yet this man could make keys by the hundred, all different, with a master key for the lot, rutting all the key wards in the key bits, with small hand tools, and without reference to any drawings. He had no need for such things he said, because he had a box of wards in his head.

The keys of many churches, chapels, public buildings, and the larger country houses, testify to the good work of those clever old key smiths.

They were not the sort of keys one could carry around in the pocket, or on a slip ring, for some of them are almost a foot long. The leading employers in the Wednesfield key trade were Thomas Mason, of Wolverhampton Road, John Mattox of Lichfield Road, and John Mattocks of Amos Lane, and there were others prominent in the industry. One notes such names as Davenport, Adey, Millichamp, Vickers, and Mason. Other trades and industries of over one hundred years ago were the manufacture of steel traps, japanned boxes and trunks.

Locks were a natural sequence to keys, and cabinet cupboard, rim, mortice, padlocks, and latches, were made in iron and brass, by such people as, Hadleys of Graisley Lane, Sam Corbett of Hickman Street, Philip Stringer of New Street, and John Powell of Lichfield Road, and there were others. Practically all lock and key smiths wore a "flag", a term applied to a bibbed white apron, which was almost the insignia of the trade concerned. Many workers went to bed in them, all the same many a new clean "flag", was pawned on a Monday to provide the means to get the owners feet in the sawdust and his hand on a pint jug.

3. Living conditions in the early 1900s

THE FAMILY, and social life of the ordinary average Wednesfield folk at the turn of the last century provides interesting, though perhaps odious, comparisons in some respects, but at the same time one feels that it meant more than seems to be the case today.

For one thing, mostly meals were a family gathering, and this to a great extent promoted a close intimacy between family members. Neighbours shared each others joys and sorrows, and also seemed to offer practical help to a much greater degree, which was a good thing, because the state did not enter into the daily life of folks, as it does these days, and of course there was no National Health and Unemployed Act.

Fig. 6. Church Street. The clock says 12.20pm, but what about the day.

Food was plain, good in the main, and unadulterated, as there were few foods canned, or preserved, so the tin opener was not the mighty weapon, or the saviour to the housewife, as it frequently is nowadays. It was a hard life generally for the average housewife, and mother. All cooking was done on, or before the open fire, in the old fashioned fire grate, or in its side oven, the old tin Dutch oven being greatly in favour for grilling bacon, ham, steak and chops, before the fire, whilst the Sunday roast would usually be seen revolving on a turn spit before the fire, operated generally by what is rarely seen now, a bright brass clockwork "Jack". Those who have not had the pleasure of eating meat, and beef cooked in that way, would not know why the praises of "The roast beef of old England", have been sung for many generations past.

Much is said today of the poverty and hunger of the bad old days, and there were certainly thin and lean times, though very few seemed to go hungry, good neighbours probably helped more than a little. Still, a satisfying meal for several could be provided for a few coppers, by a capable woman, good English boiling beef being only three pence to four pence, and the best cuts, seven pence to eight pence a pound, eggs, you could get eighteen for a shilling, rabbits, fifteen pence a couple, and there was the fact that about half the folk seemed to have a pig or more feeding up in a backyard sty, for regulations were not severe in regard to drainage, distance from dwelling houses etc. Hams, and sides of bacon were therefore familiar sights hanging from the kitchen ceiling, so one could forget butchers meat when replaced by a slice of home fed ham, or a couple of rashers of bacon, surrounded by home grown peas, and potatoes. If this does not make your mouth water, well, what will!

For be your tummy ever so tender, to such good fare it will surrender. Many folk made and baked their own bread, preparing it usually in a large earthenware "Jowl", as a large bread oven frequently formed part of the outhouses, to a row, or group of dwellings, and often a small boy, nine or ten years old would have to lug a stone, or more, of flour for the making of it, from a distant grocers shop, that was perhaps a penny or two cheaper than one round the corner. "What a hassle", you will say. Yes, indeed it was, but Oh what bread! For one can recall the appetising smell of the big hot loaves even to this day. The memories come back when you walk into a large supermarket where they bake their own bread. Frozen meat, which appeared about this time, had a very cool reception from most housewives, they called it, that, "Cag mag stuff", they considered it a real "come down", to be seen buying it. It was cheap too, for legs of frozen mutton were often

Fig. 7. View from Well Lane. Top left is the window at the Royal Oak Inn, with th[illegible] on the right. The three lads look as thought they are dressed for [illegible] school.

sold off on Saturday nights at, two shillings, to two shillings and sixpence. Of course, it eventually became accepted as being quite good to eat, but the prejudice against it died very slowly.

The average home was plainly or even barely furnished. The kitchen with the necessities, and the parlour, was often a sort of "holy of holys", with solid heavy furniture, and hand worked covers, much in fashion then. Now and then however one saw some genuine old stuff, such as Grandfather clocks, a sheep's head clock, a corner cupboard, an odd chair, or oak table, old willow pattern plates, and dishes, brass ornaments, and not forgetting the long handled copper bed warmer. These are family heir looms for the most part, but sought after now, snapped up by the antique dealer, to be sold at fancy prices, to furnish and decorate newly built, "old fashioned" type houses. In most parlour windows there was either fuchsias, geraniums, or a sweet smelling flowering, musk plant, and of course, that much maligned plant, the aspidistra, which has since provided Gracie

Fields with one of her greatest hits, "the biggest aspidistra in the world".

Clothes, for the most part, were made of materials that would wear well, and last, as they had to do, seeing that a best suit or dress would be worn in most cases for years and years. Only well-to-do-ladies could afford to go in satin and silk, for only the silk worm provided it then, but velvet was much in vogue, in lovely shades of colour, and very beautiful to us some of those dresses were. And the fashions! well, you see them shown at the cinema now and then, but how our bright young women today shriek at the mere idea of wearing of strong whale-boned corset (stays), tightly laced, to create a tiny waist, that two hands could almost span, high necked tight fitting bodice, with puff leg of mutton type long sleeves, and a flounced skirt, that swept the floor, gathering all the dust and dirt. Yes, a woman was hardly considered to be respectable dressed otherwise. All this was usually crowned by a large hat trimmed with ribbons, artificial flowers, feathers, birds wings, and even complete wild birds, which were caught by the thousands, and processed for this purpose.

Things of wonder some of those hats were. But they were disastrous to wild bird life, all bird lovers were thankful when that fashion died out.

For men, a black coat and vest, with grey striped trousers, and the inevitable bowler, or "billycock", as it was often called. It was considered to be the thing, but was rarely worn except for special occasions.

Children's clothes were a problem, for mothers especially, as families tended to be rather larger than nowadays, so of real necessity many small garments were made from the cast off clothing of elders, by the industrious mother, who had to make-do-and-mend at all times, knit socks, and stockings, mufflers, and those hundred and one things, in which perhaps lies the origin, of that well known saying, a woman's work is never done.

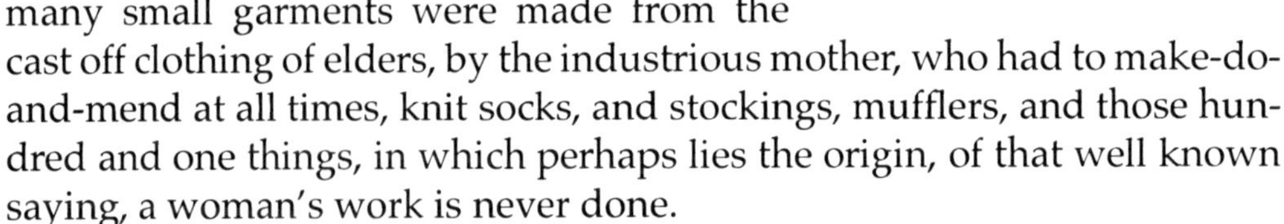

The husband, besides his daily occupation, usually ten hours, or even more in some cases, generally had a bit of garden to do, grow vegetables, clean the pigsty out, and a few other odd jobs, before he settled down to a rest, with perhaps a drink of home brew from the "Local", and a bit of bread and cheese, also a smoke no doubt, if things ran to it. A few had a hobby such as pigeon racing, or maybe a whippet was kept, whilst some played bowls. Quiet lives on the whole, but few suffered from headaches, or nervous ailments as today. A pig-killing was one of the high spots in the lives of youngsters, and lads always seemed to know of such events pending, they would contrive to be there if possible, because of the odd chance the pig might get loose and run amok amidst great excitement, and if it was a big bacon pig, it took several men to recapture him, and hold him down on the bench, whilst the pig killer cut its throat, and the victim expired slowly with agonised, but ever weakening, squeals. Most boys revelled in the proceedings with a sort of unholy joy, whilst girls, and many women too, shut themselves up in the houses, this was because many of the women often fed the pigs, and gave each a name, to which they would give an answering grunt, so they got quite upset on the day of execution.

All the same, the boys themselves were filled with fear at the gory figure of one pig killer in particular, in his leather belt, and murderous long sheaf knife. Then there was the cutting up of the carcass, preparing the chitterlings, rendering down the fat to make the Rosemary flavoured lard, with its residue of savoury scratchings, which provided extra work for days afterwards for the good wife, in which kindly neighbours lent a helping hand. The curing of hams and bacon is an art, so when the hams and sides of bacon were ready, the expert services of old Mr George Lane, of New Street, were sought by many folk.

Candles, and paraffin lamps of the table, wall and hanging types, provided light in most homes, although plain gas lights could be seen in many shops, and other business premises, but when the incandescent gas mantle appeared soon after, it threw quite a different light on things.

Electricity for lighting purposes was as yet in its infancy, as regards its use for and by the general public.

Coal was good, plentiful, and cheap, perhaps too cheap, for the miner often worked under bad conditions, and though a few appeared to do fairly well, the money should no doubt have been more, for it is at all times a hazardous occupation. A load of good Holly Bank House coal was delivered by local hauliers for fifteen shillings and sixpence, and it was mostly near 21 hundred weight, cobbles and nuts of coal were about 13 shillings and sixpence, slack for furnaces, and workshop stoves was about nine shillings to ten shillings, all delivered, prices which seem utterly ridiculous these days.

There was no resident doctor in Wednesfield at that time, and any illness meant a journey to Willlenhall or Heath Town, which, at night, especially in snow and sleet during winter, was no light matter, and a lantern was often carried on such journeys.

4. Wednesfield inns and innkeepers

"THE INN", two words associated with all grades of people for many centuries past, and imprinted on our infant minds too, since the birth of Jesus two thousand years ago, in the stable at Bethlehem, because there was "No room at the Inn". Then the Good Samaritan took the traveller, robbed and wounded, to an inn to be cared for, because the inn primarily existed to provide food and shelter for man and beast, night and day.

Such accommodation was limited in the middle ages, since many travellers found food and shelter at monasteries, and abbeys, no doubt also at less cost, but that was before Henry VIII robbed and despoiled these religious places. Roadside alehouses were common, but served only, as did the wine shop of early Roman and Greek times for a cup of wine and a gossip, probably about chariot races, or wild beast fights. Just as today, many drop in at the local pub for a pint and chat about current events; indeed, this is the chief business of the publican.

At the turn of the last century scarcely one of the about twenty inns of that time, could provide bed and board for a traveller, though some could stable a horse or two, and provide a meal, but full board meant Wolverhampton, whose close proximity, was probably why Wednesfield's inns did not cater fully, for the bona fide traveller.

There were obviously too many inns, or more correctly, public houses, over a hundred years ago, because there are no more now in 2009, even with a vast increase in population. Indeed, many have ceased trading, recently - The Crown, Nordley Hill, now demolished, and the new building is a nursing home; The Wood Hayes, Woodend Road; The Falcon, March End; and at the time of writing The Pheasant, has closed and has been boarded up. Also The Prestwood Arms has ceased trading.

The well-conducted village inn played a big part in social life then, not as a drinking den, but as a place where villagers of all grades met, to exchange views, and maybe have a song, for theatres were few and no cinemas existed.

A little wine must must be good for us, otherwise our Lord would not have performed his first miracle, by turning water into wine, at the marriage feast at Cana in Galilee, whilst the Psalmist, David, also sings its praises. However, the Bible records instances where strong drink was much abused also, and usually the customer and not the publican is the sinner. Certainly, the cheerful warmth, and almost homely welcome encouraged customers to linger by the big fire on cold nights, for coal was very cheap then, and more than one pub kitchen was a cheerful picture, with red tiled floor, tables and benches white with scrubbing, shining brasses hanging alongside the chimney piece.

Yes, the seats were hard, but the atmosphere was not.

The Dog and Partridge

The oldest house in Wednesfield is the "Dog and Partridge", at the turn of the last century the landlord was John Gregory, called "Tom" by his intimate friends.

The Dog and Partridge has stood on its present site for hundreds of years. No one really knows how long, but its the same basic structure today, as it was in 1840, with no major alterations having taken place up until the 1990s, in fact its most likely that this pub is one of the two ale houses that existed in Wednesfield, in the 1600s, the other one was most likely The Pheasant. Nearby, Pinfold Bridge is more commonly known as Gregorys Bridge, Gregory is said to have never let the fire go out, winter or summer.

6.00am until 11.00pm, were the hours in those days, not good in many ways, but appreciated by some early workers on a raw cold morning, for they could get two pennyworth of hot rum and coffee, which was good for the asthmatic, and those with bad colds.

Such a two penn'orth costs quite a lot more nowadays and you cannot get it on the way to work, early mornings. Mulled ale was in demand on very cold nights, the muller, a copper funnel shape vessel, was thrust into the fire, ale poured in, with ginger and sugar added, as it warmed up. It also warmed the customers up.

Regulars calling for a morning glass about 11.30am or so, were invited to bread and cheese, maybe pickles too, a generous gesture, spoilt by some who made a meal of it, with their one and half glass of beer.

At one time tithe feasts were held at the Dog, farmers, and many well known people would come to pay their tithes there. They would have a feast, with many game birds, and beef and pork to choose from, many of the hungry farmers would just keep eating, until they could not eat an-

Fig. 8. The Dog and Partridge Inn 1956/57. Notice the houses that have been demolished. By the lady pushing the pushchair was The Lion; Woolworths was later built on the back gardens.

other morsel, and therefore these tithe feasts became very popular at the Dog and Partridge.

Harry Gregory

With the passing of Mr Harry Gregory on Wednesday February 13th 1957 in his 89th year, we lost one of the oldest, and perhaps best known of Wednesfield's inhabitants, for he was born here, and lived here throughout his very long life. He was the eldest son of the late Mr John Gregory, and was of course, closely associated with the Dog and Partridge, in the High Street, which has been the home of the Gregory family for over 100 years, most of them born and raised here, and where for many years Harry brewed the ale.

His greatest pride and interest, however, was in the old bowling green, the preparation of which, with its surrounding trimly cut and shaped hedges was a great joy to him, and a labour of love.

A fine bowls player himself, he was amongst the few who were directly responsible for the formation of the Staffordshire Crown Green Bowling

Association; Gregory's green being one of the oldest in South Staffordshire, whilst its old club was famed throughout the country, then for its brilliant performances, winning the Staffordshire Challenge Cup, many times, and Harry Gregory had a big part in the success and fame the club achieved. The present landlords at the time of writing are Mr and Mrs Cox. They keep a good pint of Banks beer and serve some tasty food, at very reasonable prices. There is an extension being built at the rear, with its completion the Dog and Partridge will be able to cater for more customers.

Where the extension is being built, an old water pump stands, it is very old and must date back to those tithe feasts.

Wolverhampton and Dudley Breweries purchased the Dog and Partridge in 1963 from the Gregorys, the pub still retains the atmosphere of an old, quaint inn, with its fireplace, and old original oak beams.

The old pump has been incorporated into the extension and its now a feature in the Dog and Partridge.

Other inns and innkeepers of Wednesfield were, Will Hadley at the Star, New Street, who was also a trap maker, and famous breeder of racing pigeons. He was invited to Sandringham house once, for advice, in King Edward VII's time, as he had a famous loft too.

Rotund and Rosy Ned Hadley were lower down New Street at the Talbot with John Brooks, big and bluff, at the Albion, opposite.

In Rookery Street, Harry (Masher) Vann, kept the New Inns, whilst at the Pyle Back, there was the distinguished looking John Wilcox, who had a bevy of handsome daughters. Will Taffley - "Old Taff" to so many - had the Old Crown, Church Street.

There was the Williams family at The Boat, the Warners at the Angel, Lewis at the Red Lion, and already mentioned John Gregory at the Dog and Partridge.

The Pyle Cock, Rookery Street, was a Banks' house, it has been around since 1868. The Cock has had recent alterations at the rear. You can find some old regulars in there early in the morning soon after opening time.

The Royal Tiger, High Street

The Royal Tiger has stood on its present site since 1875, Thomas Howe was licensee before 1908, and he remained until the early 1920s.

The photograph taken sometime around 1908 shows Muriel Howe on the right and Sarah Howe on the left.

The Tiger was then home brewed beer as can be seen on the sign.

The sign on the Tiger has been mistaken for a clock in past photographs, but on this photograph you can see that it is an advertising sign for home brewed beer, the building to the left of the Tiger, is thought by some, to be the house where a mother and daughter perished in a fire.

Previous keepers of the Tiger were Clement Jones in the 1880s and James Howard Warner in the 1920s.

The Boat, Church Street

The Boat has not been altered much over the years, although it has recently had an extension added to it.

Around 1915 the licensee was a W.J. Gumbley, but in the 1920s the licence was in Mrs Gumbley's name.

The Cross Guns, Lichfield Road

The Cross Guns like the Vine used to stand on the front of the main road, it was rebuilt at the rear of the old one in the 1930s. Past landlords have included: Joshua Hope 1845, he must have been one of the first landlords. Thomas Lewis 1880s; Thomas Griffiths 1920s and Arthur Hadley, and later Phil and Jill Smith.

The Cross Guns can be seen on the 1891 O.S. map of Wednesfield.

The photograph showing a gathering of well known people of Wednesfield ready to embark on a breakfast trip to Stourport around the late 1950s.

There are some well known faces in this picture, but sadly many of them are no longer with us. Can you recognise anyone in the picture? A few should be able to remember - Buzzer Morgan, Spadger Potts, and his brother Cash, Gommie Lovatt of Tithe Road, Fred Thompson, and the man himself, Arthur Hadley. These trips were very common in the 1950s and 1960s. Other pubs of Wednesfield did similar trips, perhaps you went on one? In those days men could have their fill, and remain gentlemen, the same cannot be said today!

The Angel Inn, High Street

Friday, December 5th 1958, is a day remembered with some sadness in Wednesfield, for on that date the Angel, the last home brewed house in Wednesfield, and one of the last in the country, served its last pint of home brewed beer.

The licensee of this well known High Street inn, Mr James Howe, retired from the business he took over when his father died in 1932. One of his first acts as landlord was to have the interior of the house largely rebuilt and modernised, a fact that contributed in no small way to the popularity the Angel, enjoyed during his term as host.

Fig. 9. The Boat in c1915.

Mr Howe had a worthy partner in his wife, and together they made the inn, a centre of social activities in the district.

In 1952 the Angel, was made the headquarters of Wednesfield public bowls club, with Jim Howe acting as secretary.

Previous Licensees were, 1850s Luke Marshal, late 1880s William Warner, and in the 1920s Thos. Howe.

The Rose and Crown, High Street

The Rose and Crown, was flanked by Frost Chemist, and Downings the butchers. A nickname for the Rose and Crown was, "Vinny Austins", it was a Butlers house, the Crown was demolished in the 1960s, previous licensees were Francis Peace 1840s, W. Green 1850s, Thos. Brindley 1880s, and Thomas Banks 1920s.

The Vine, Lichfield Road

The Vine was originally closer to the main road up until 1939, when the present Vine was built at the rear of the old one; they then demolished the old Vine.

Fig.11. On the right is the Angel Inn with T Howe on the sign he had. The Angel in the 1920s, Dones the baker is two doors up. Notice the height of the church wall. It must be at least seven feet high; I wonder why?

The Vine was a Truemans house until the 1970s it then changed to Courage beers. Mrs Florence Cocking was licensee in the 1920s, and later her daughter Floss Lathe, who was born in the Vine on the 14th of June 1928. Floss took over the licence in 1956.

The Old Crown, Church Street

I don't think that many of you will remember this pub. It was situated just past where the Library stands today. There were a couple of houses that used to stand on the site of the Library. I believe that at one time, the occupants of those two houses were the Bodley, and Wallbank families; Mary Bodley used to live there.

The Old Crown closed in 1926/ 1927, the licence was transferred to the newly built public house on the Nordley Hill Estate, The New Crown, which opened for trade in 1927, the date can be found under the eaves of the building, at the time of writing, the New Crown has now been demolished. Some previous licensees of the Old Crown were, J Marshall 1850s, Benjamin Corbett 1880s, and Thos. Adey 1920s, Paddy Weir was one of the

Fig.10. Bunting cobblers hut on the left. Jack Howes friut and veg next door. Then Barclays Bank, the 59 Wednesfield Bus. On the right The Rose and Crown in c1961; the pub had already closed down.

Fig.12. Back of the shops in Church Street, said to have been where the Old Crown Inn stood. It is now a carpark. Photograph is from 1989.

landlords of the New Crown.

The Albion, New Street

The Albion stood in New Street next to Tomlinsons newsagents, lower down towards the Wolverhampton road. Previous landlords were John Tonks 1840s to 1850s, John Brooks 1880s, and Harry White 1920s.

The Talbot, New Street

Yet another pub in New Street, the Talbot, was across the road from the Albion. Landlords were Edward Mason 1880s, Rotund and Rosy Ned Hadley 1900s.

New Street as you well know was on the Hickman estate, this estate which consisted of New, North, Cross, Charles, and Hickman Streets. These streets were demolished in the name of progress, which came in the shape of three multi storey flats, and some houses. Give me those old streets anytime rather than those flats!

The Royal Oak, Rookery Street

The Royal Oak stood on the corner of Rookery Street and Well Lane, it was a Butlers house, some of the past landlords were: George Roberts 1880s, Frank Thompson mid 1920s, and J. Seeding in the 1850s, Polly Mason was connected with the Royal Oak for well over 50 years.

The New Inns, Rookery Street

The New Inns stood at the top of Rookery Street, just about in front of Sidebothams, the trap makers. The New Inns was similar in appearance to the Dog and Partridge, it had the same wooden rails outside, they must have been there to tether horses to. The ale at one time was Atkins, Atkinsons Brewery Ltd, was taken over by Mitchells and Butlers in 1959, this brewery was eventually demolished in 1969. Some past landlords of the New Inns have been John Tomkys mid 1840s until the mid 1850s, Harry Wearing 1880s, and Samuel Foster 1920s. The New Inns' nickname was "Sammy Frankie".

Other public houses

Some other public houses and their past landlords were:-

The Noahs Ark. John Moorwood mid 1840s. W. Haywood 1850s.

The Falcon, March End. Thomas Morris 1880s. Walter MacLachan 1920s. And George Thomas.

The Castle Inn, Wood End. Mrs Sarah Anne Harper 1880s. John Edward Southall 1920s, who retired in the early 1950s.

The Pheasant, Wood End. William Marston 1880s. William Henry Pritchard 1920s, and Mrs Lydia Mason, who was very well known and respected. She vacated the house on July 8th 1954, moving to Long Knowle with her brother Jack Wooton.

The Pear Tree, Scotlands. John Sadler 1850s. Robert Groves 1880s. Bert Adey 1930s to 1959, and William Henry Humphreys 1920s.

The Royal Oak, Scotlands. T. Smith 1850s. Charles Everall 1880s, and William Henry Mincher 1920s.

The Lion, High Street, across the road from the Royal Tiger. R. Williams 1920s.

The Star was at the top of New Street, not very far from the fish shop. Ansells were later the brewery that supplied the beer, past landlords were Harry Davenport 1920s, and Rose and Jack Morgan during the War years.

Social clubs

June 1960 saw contractors move onto the site at Linthouse Lane to build a new pub opposite Kitchen Lane. Mr Cyril Downing was the steward of the

Fig.15. This Photograph of 1934 tells its own story.

What a year! What do you recall of that year?

Figures.16 . The Vine (top), and The Cross Guns (bottom), in c1895. A man and a small child stand in the doorway of The Vine with The Cross Guns further up the road. In the 1930s the two pubs were rebuilt behind the buildings in the photograph. They then simply demolished the old buildings leaving the new pubs with a nice carpark at the front. Although the photograph was taken in around 1895 there does not appear to be any sign of Taylor Street.

Fig.14. On the left is The Star, looking down towards Wolverhampton road, in c1927. Blowers fish and chip shop is lower down the road, also a drapers.

Fig.13. Between the two buses you can see The Royal Oak, corner of Well Lane and Rookery Street. The man standing to the right of the picture is said to have been Mr Pallant.

Fig.17. This is a trip to Stourport from the Cross Guns in the 1950s.

There are some well known faces in this picture.

PEAR
TREE
INN.
BUTLERS
ALES
WINES
AND
SPIRITS

Civil Defence Club, his assistant was Mr J.T. Bowen. Can you recall where the Civil Defence Club stood?

Wednesfield Social Club, Bolton House, Bolton Road. In the 1950s the membership fees were males 2/3 pence and females 1/3 pence. The club was formed in 1936, and in 1953 the membership stood at nearly 800, amenities in 1953 included snooker, darts, dominoes, bowls and crib. Each section having a team for various leagues. The Club was later extended and therefore lost the bowling green.

Fig.43. (Opposite, top). The Pear Tree Inn on the Cannock Road, a semi country house, prior to its demolition in 1937.

Fig. 42. The Pear Tree Inn. The wagon and horses were hired from Billy Smart's Circus for some function that was about to take place. Bert Adey, sports promoter was licensee of this inn from the 1930s to 1959. See the Sports chapter.

Fig.19. The Pyle Cock Inn, taken in 1990. This pub has stood on this site since c1868.

5. Shops and traders

SHOPS of Wednesfield. There were lots, and there still are today. I am going to mention quite a few.

Dones the Bakers. This shop in the High Street has been turning out bread since 1867, the current address is 41 High Street, the old number would probably have been 21. The cobblers in the High Street. It was a wooden hut. Mr Buntin was the cobbler he celebrated his 50th wedding anniversary, you probably remember it was next to Jack Howes' fruit & veg shop.

Pickerings newsagents and hairdressers stood next to the Wesleyan church at the Rookery bend, corner of Well Lane, but the shop actually started off across the road, it changed from Pickerings to

Fig.18. Wednesfield Social Club Bowls Team and Club Bowlers, taken c1954. Do you see anyone you know?

Charlesworth in 1957, I used to take papers for Charlesworth in the early 1960s. Pickerings shop was established in Wednesfield village in 1896.

Hubbles the barbers shop stood close to the chemists in the High Street, Frosts, or was it Roses? or could it have been Patersons - all three had been the chemists at one time or another.

J.V. Trubshaw, a corner shop on High Street and Neachells lane, was a watch and clock repairs, also jewellery, and it also sold sweets. This shop still stands today. Do you know what kind of business it is today?

There used to be about six houses along the side of this shop. They ran right up to the canal, the little shop does not look very old, does it? You will be surprised to learn it was there in the 1920s.

Sambrokes, Butcher, Lichfield Road, next to Frankie Griffiths the greengrocer shop - do you remember Frank? - he used to make home made faggots and paes in gravy, all you needed was a jug to carry it in.

Frank used to be a keen pigeon fancier, his pigeon loft was at the bottom of his garden, and just by it stood a lovely apple tree; I know it was a lovely apple tree, because I used to go scrumping there many times.

Another butcher was R. Lovatt, his premises were 20 High Street, only a couple of doors from Downings Butchers shop. Lewis, another butcher opposite the Pyle Cock in Rookery Street.

Pete the Pirate, grocer of 46 High Street, also at 52 New Street and later opened a shop in Rookery Street. A young child was killed outside the High Street shop. I believe that a lorry came down Gregorys bridge and lost control, a tragic accident.

A. Crutchley, 19 Moat House Lane West; flowers for all occasions.

Robinsons greengrocer, Lichfield Road, later a fishing tackle shop and also a betting office at one time, run by Norman Round.

C. Morris, hairdresser, 115 Lichfield Road, just over Wards Bridge on the left.

Millards grocers, Lichfield Road, later Audreys School Uniforms.

J. Round, watch and jewellery repairs, situated on the corner of Hickman

Fig.21. In this photograph you can see that Barclays Bank had not yet been built. But it looks like the houses that were there have been demolished ready for a new building. Barclays was built in 1957/58.

and New Streets.

In the 1950s Wednesfield Laundry, a 24 hours bag wash cost 3/6d. for an 18 pound wash, at their address in Cross Street.

Norgroves, fruit and veg, High Street. Powells had the same shop.

T.S.B. moved from the Rookery bend at 5 High Street, to its new address, Church Street, in 1964.

The official opening of the first house on the Long Knowle Estate took place on Tuesday the 8th of September 1953. Wednesfield's own T.A. unit, took over the Drill Hall opposite the Vine, 1955.

Walter Downing, 16 High Street

The name of Downing has been associated with farming and butchering, for several generations, and there has been a Downings family, at the High Street address for over a century. Old John Downing was a butcher there

Fig.20. The chemists next to the T.V. shop. I think you can just see the name of Frosts above. Across the road is Buntings' hut, the cobblers, next door to Howes fruit and veg shop. The photograph was taken in c1960.

over a century ago, but sad to say he is no longer with us. His brother, Harry who had a butchers shop in Heath Town, eventually took over, and later handed the High Street shop to Walter his son in about 1919, and whilst his father Harry lived to the ripe old age of 94, and was active at that, Walter died at a comparatively early age in 1938, leaving his wife and son (another Walter), only eleven years old, to carry on.

She made a courageous fight to keep going all through the War years,

helped by of course her son Walter. They also had a branch shop at Nordley Hill, which opened in 1932, they sold this shop in the 1950s, because Mrs Downing found it too much for her and Walter to do justice to the shops, because they had also other business interests in a smallholding, which took up a lot of time and attention.

Walter used to put up many orders for delivery to customers, and very tempting they used to look too, proving that Downings fully merited the reputation they built up, for good quality meat at reasonable prices. The cheerful personality of Mrs Downing, and the courteous attention given to all customers by her son, no doubt accounted for the prosperity of the business, but it's sad that, it's a Wednesfield High Street now, without a Downings shop, one of the old Wednesfield family names.

Allan Bennett's Butcher's, High Street

Allan Bennett's Butcher's shop has been in Wednesfield for more than 30 years. In the last ten years it has been run by Paul and Dawn Riley.

It has been run as a traditional local butcher where quality is the main priority.

Fig.22. J. Downings, the butchers, 16 High Street. This is a very early photograph. To the right is the Rose and Crown Inn. The picture is c1905. All the slaughtering was done at the rear of the premises. Is the lad anyone you know?

Fig.23. Rookery Street shops. To the right, is where Squire's hardware used to be. To the left stood the Royal Oak Inn. I believe these four shops were going to be re-erected at the Black Country Museum.

Paul and Dawn are committed to preserving the skills passed down through many generations of traditional craftsmen. Their products are made using only top quality British meat from local farmers. This means low food miles. Over the years they have won both regional and national competitions with their sausages. They were National Sausage Champions 2008. From their prize winning best pork sausage, to their pork and leek, and Old English sausage, yes! it's true to say that you would have to travel far to find such excellent sausages produced on the premises at the High Street shop.

Also all of their cooked meats are made on the premises. This ensures high standards can be maintained. The traditional boiled ham, and even roast beef are firm favourites. A variety of meat and fruit pies are baked daily to ensure freshness. Their own produced black pudding, has also won numerous competitions.

In addition, Paul and Dawn can provide a buffet service for all occasions with free local delivery.

All in all, Bennetts' offer first class produce at very keen prices. The proof of the pudding is in the eating! I should know, I shop there. Well done, Paul and Dawn for providing, Wednesfield with such excellent products where quality and freshness are never surpassed.

Anslow's Shop, Nordley Road

Can you remember Anslow's shop in Nordley Road? One person who can is Sylivia Parry, she worked there in the late 1950s.

Sylvia was born in Nordley Road. At the aged of seven she moved into Woden Avenue where she lived with Mum and Dad until she was 18. She then joined the Land Army and in 1943 moved to North Wales. Sylvia's maiden name was Creswell, she married Hugh in 1947 at St Thomas' Church. Hugh worked for 40 years at New Cross Hospital. Sylvia still lives in Wednesfield over on the Moat House Estate. One of her friends and a neighbour of the days when they lived in Nordley Road is Ann Hunt. She does not live in Wednesfield anymore; she moved to Wolverhampton.

Post Office, High Street

Alfred Squire, who died in 1956 at the age of 93, lived at the Hills, Lichfield Road, he was the local postmaster at the old shop that stood on the corner of Bealeys Fold.

In the days when Mr Squire ran the shop over 90 years ago, it was an independent sub post office, which included all the usual counter work, telegraph (morse), and three daily collections, deliveries, and despatches, but only one on a Sunday. Mr Squire also had a musical shop in the village at one time.

Older inhabitants, alive today, will remember the other post office further up the High Street.

The earliest reference in the post office title deeds reveals that in 1792 two cottages known as Lavenders tenements, stood on this land, the cottages were occupied by a John Pedley, and a William Perry.

The names and occupations of some of the owners of the land from 1792 to 1886, are shown as Thomas Kempson, 'yeoman', Richard Phillips of Bushbury, Richard Hadley of Wednesfield coffin handle makers, and Mary Tomkys, innkeeper.

An interesting fact about the building is that it was conveyed to a Cornelius Constable in 1890 for £80, Leonard Broomhall purchased the building in 1914. This was then run as a post office by Mr Broomhall and his wife.

On an autumn morning in 1921, a young lad, fresh from school, stood before the shop in the High Street. For him it was a great occasion, he was about to start his first job, telegraph boy, under his father Leonard, the boy was of course Stanley.

Over the years Stanley Broomhall saw great changes and an enormous increase in the volume of post office business. In his early days, Westcroft seemed to have far more than its fair share of telegrams, and it was nothing unusual for him to travel there on foot, four or five times in a single day.

Time passed, the young man used it to learn every aspect of the work, and on the death of his mother in 1935, he became postmaster, whilst his wife took over the ladies, and children's outfitters, that made up the other half of the family business.

Stanley Broomhall became chairman of the council of social services, chairman of the old peoples welfare committee, and president of the old peoples friendship club. As a member of Wednesfield Urban District Council, he was Vice Chairman (1948-1951) and Chairman from 1951 to 1953; a high office which he held with great distinction, and from which he gained considerable esteem and respect. But of all his work, perhaps the nearest to his heart, was that for the old folks, and under his guidance, amenities for Wednesfield's old people have certainly been enormously extended.

It was through the payment of old age pensions that Stanley first became interested in old people and their problems.

In 1934 he and his wife organised the first of the outings for Wednesfield's old people, which from then on became an annual event.

The new post office that stands today was built at the rear of the old one, Mr and Mrs Broomhall moved into the new post office on the 21st of October 1959.

The Broomhalls retired from the post office business at the end of March 1961. Incidentally, the building was designed by their daughter who was an architect, Mrs Margaret Campbell.

It is recorded that in 1851 the postmaster for Wednesfield was a Mr John Hope.

Hylda Baker opens new High Street shop

The rapidly expanding Birmingham family business of Sam Carpenter and Sons Limited, opened their 24th Midlands radio and television shop at 7 High Street on Tuesday June 6th 1961.

Popular comedienne Hylda Baker, travelled from Birmingham to perform the opening ceremony. After cutting a white ribbon across the doorway of the bright and modern new shop she was received by the chairman of Wednesfield Urban District Council (Councillor A.D. Griffiths) and Mrs Griffiths, and by Vice Chairman (Councillor Arthur Johnson) and Mrs Johnson.

Housewives paused from the afternoon shopping to

crowd round the shop doorway, chatting to Hylda Baker and collecting her autograph.

Sisters honoured

Special guests at the opening ceremony were two elderly sisters, Miss A Thews, and Miss E Thews, of 2 Mattox Road. They were chosen by Councillor Griffiths as having spent a lifetime working for others in need, to receive a handsome television set, given by the company to mark the opening of the shop.

On hearing that the sisters were anxious to see the wedding of the Duke of Kent on television, Mr Sam Carpenter and his brother Neville made arrangements to have the set installed at the sisters home in time for the event.

Woolworths opened in the High Street on the 28th of August 1964. It doesn't seem quite that long ago, particularly as this year (2009) it has now closed: Woolworths out of business, who'd have believed it!

Joe Crutchley opened his Woodend service station also in 1964.

D.H. Woods of Rookery Street was established in the village in the early 1920s.

Fig.24. Sam Carpenters' shop on the left. This looks like it is just before its opening in June 1961.

Fig.25 (right). Joseph Swatman's barbers, High Street. You can see the barber's pole above the door. The picture is taken in c1912. This shop was very similar to the one in Church Street. Joseph was seventeen at the time of the photograph.

Fig. 26 (opposite). This photograph is more clear. Would you let him cut your hair, or give you a shave? Look at the top right of the image, what is it?

The row of shops by the side of The Regal, sorry I mean the supermarket, were built in 1949, these were owned by Mr P. Swatman, now Nat West Bank, and the pet shop.

The welfare clinic in Alfred Squire Road opened in 1960.

Swatman's, the barbers

A well-known shop in the village at the turn of the last century was Swatman's, the barbers.

Joseph Swatman was a barber, and his shop was at number 29 High Street

next door to B. Oaks, the butchers, Joseph's brother John had his shop at 7 Church Street. Joseph's shop later became a hardware shop.

There were five Swatman brothers in all, and one of the brothers, P. Swatman, owned those couple of shops by The Regal, at one time they were a cafe and a wool shop, later to be a pet shop and Nat West. Another Wednesfield barber was Mr Pickering, who retired from active business in 1951.

He became an apprentice to the trade at the early age of 10. At 18 he was the manager of Peters hairdressing salon, Wolverhampton.

In 1896 he commenced business in his native town of Wednesfield, by opening No. 3 High Street, as a hairdressers, also No. 5 as a general dealers shop. During later years he transferred his business, across the road, to No. 2, where his son, Eric, and daughter Vera, who were each qualified hairdressers, carried on the business which he had pioneered. His other son Leslie, was also connected with the hairdressing trade, and held high appointments in that sphere.

In 1920 Mr Pickering was elected to serve as a member of the council. He served in this capacity, with great interest, until he retired from public life in 1946.

His retirement was unfortunate, but was inevitable, because of heavy commitments to his expanding business. During his earlier years, Mr Pickering, was secretary of St Thomas Church Bible Class, holding this position from 1908 until 1926.

The two barbers that I have mentioned, both started off as barbers, but which one of them was the first? Or could there have been another to lay claim to this, do you know?

I don't know about the High Street, but there was a Tom Mason, who did his barbering at Hickman Street, many, many years ago.

Another barber in the early 1960s was Cyril Morris of 115 Lichfield Road. Also a ladies hairstyling shop was Elizabeths of Wednesfield, at 37b Lichfield Road, opposite the school and near to the Cross Guns, that was in 1964.

Wednesfield traders, early 1920s

Fredk, Walt Baker.	butcher.	31 High Street
Walter Downing.	butcher.	16 High Street
William Henry Hill.	butcher.	68 Rookery Street
James William Hulme.	butcher.	70 to 74 Rookery Street and 11 New Street
Miss Maud Nicholls.	pork butcher.	20 High Street

William Sanders Quinton.	butcher.	21 New Street
Miss Ada Tew.	pork butcher.	15 Well Lane
Fredk Bailey.	baker.	12 Hickman Street
Thomas Arnold Biddulph.	baker.	Rookery Street
Jas Bristow.	boot repairer.	14 March End
Samuel Dudley.	boot repairer.	33 New Street
Mrs Sarah Ecclestone.	boot and shoe dealer.	28 Rookery Street
Frank Harris.	boot repairer.	25 Rookery Street
Joseph Norwood.	boot repairer.	17 Well Lane
Harry Thompson.	book maker.	9 High Street
Josiah Hyde.	manufacturing chemist.	High Street
Alexander Paterson.	chemist.	21 Rookery Street
Mrs Beatrice Rose.	drug stores.	12 High Street
Mrs Kate Bellamy.	draper.	43 Wolverhampton Road
Thomas Collis.	draper.	24 High Street
Mrs Gertrude Birch.	dairy.	78 Graisley Lane
Vincent Hyde.	farmer Moat Farm, dairyman.	Bolton Road
Sam Adey.	greengrocer.	7 High Street
Thomas Beech.	grocer.	27 Wolverhampton Road, Wood End
Walter Chaplin.	grocer.	26 High Street
Richard Dodd.	grocer.	Wood End
Jas Done.	grocer.	19 High Street
Frederick Giles.	grocer.	52 New Street
Mrs Emily Harris.	grocer.	Rookery Street
Chas Hubball.	grocer.	29 Lichfield Road
John Jones.	grocer.	Vicarage Road
George Lewis.	grocer.	58 Rookery Street
Charles Wooton.	grocer.	33 High Street
James Hinton.	greengrocer and fruiterer.	25 New Street
John Anslow.	shopkeeper.	Wood End
Albert Banks.	shopkeeper.	131 March End
Mrs Marion Bennett.	"' .	63 Hart Road
Edward Bradley.	"' .	84 Graisley Lane
Alfred Cashmore.	"' .	11 Neachells Lane

Thos Cooper.	"	.	Wood End
William Corbett.	"	.	21 Hart Road
Thos Crutchley.	"	.	Wood End
Wm Davies.	"	.	105 Neachells Lane
Mrs Martha Dixon.	"	.	100 Graisley Lane
Thos Dudley.	"	.	31 New Street
Wm Bert Evans.	"	.	32 High Street
Thos Lewis.	"	.	9 Church Street
Mrs Naomi Perks.	"	.	11 Cross Street
Miss Alice Pinches.	"	.	Wood End
Wm Hy Riley.	"	.	150 March End
Mrs Ada Robinson.	"	.	Vicarage Road
Francis Robinson.	"	.	March End
Mrs Rebecca Rose.	"	.	22 New Street

Fig.27. Pickerings on the corner of Well Lane. Barclays Bank is on the left next door to the Pelham Steam Laundry. The Regal cinema can just be seen by the Wesleyan Church, next to Pickerings, prior to 1957.

Thomas Salt.	" .	46 High Street
John Swift.	" .	69 Bloxwich Road
Benjamin Turner.	" .	20 Hart Road
Mrs Mary Wood.	" .	62 Rookery Street
Mrs Mary Edge.	confectioner.	62 New Street
Mrs Edith Fisher.	pawnbroker.	33 Church Street
Mrs Genevra Hill.	pawnbroker.	3 Rookery Street
Frederick Jackson.	hairdresser.	1 Hall Street
Albert Rose.	newsagent.	8 High Street
John Swatman.	hairdresser.	7 Church Street
Isaac Tomlinson.	newsagent.	13 New Street
William James Leeding.	fishmonger.	27 Rookery Street
Thomas Nicholls.	fried fish shop.	37 Rookery Street
Mrs Annie Rudler.	fishmonger.	29 Wolverhampton Road

Fig.28. Wootons, grocer, seed merchant, next door to B. Oaks & Son, butchers, in 1944. S.R. Bayley purchased the premises. The address was 33 High Street.

A few farmers around the early 1920s

Ralph Alcock.	Wolverhampton Road
Joseph Downing.	Wood End
H.W.&J. Ecclestone.	Perry Hall Farm
Vincent Hyde.	Moat Farm
Richard Henry Lewis.	Bridge Farm, Lichfield Road
Mrs Mary Ann Pinches.	Wood Hayes Farm
John Simpson.	Shed Farm
Ernest Smith.	Prestwood Farm, Wood End
Frederick Thornley.	Ashmore Park
Vincent Bradburn.	cowkeeper. Long Knowle
Mrs Elizabeth Wooton.	cowkeeper. Wood End

Coal merchants

Joseph Foulkes.	Victoria Wharf, Wolverhampton Road

Fig.29. Dones, the bakers, in about 1900.

Thomas Grosvenor. Noose Lane
Zachariah & Ernest Pursehouse.
New Cross Wharf
Harold Williams. Bridge Wharf, Graisley Lane

Wednesfield had at this time no fewer than:-
11 trap makers, 7 lock makers, and 22 key makers
Mr William Edward was a cycle repairer at Pinfold Bridge.
Mr Richard Arkinstall was blacksmith in Long Knowle Lane.
Bayliss and Wilson were stamper and piecers in Bealeys Fold.
A Henry Lane Ltd (established 1844) of Eagle Works, was a manufacturer of every kind of steel vermin traps.

Purshouse & Gregory were builders based in the High Street near to Glens fruit shop. A Mr Frank Johnson had refreshment rooms at 57 Well Lane, and Mr Walter Reginald Pumfrey was Wednesfield station master.

B.S. Done & Son, 41 High Street, Wednesfield

Bakers, confectioners and grocers, birthday cakes, and wedding cakes, made as required, home baked bread, rolls and cakes. Grocery orders collected and delivered, telephone W.ton 31746. That's the advert they put in the Wolverhampton Chronicle March 7th 1967.

A small family bakery and grocers in Wednesfield, celebrated its centenary in 1967.

The owner Mr Wallace Done inherited the firm from his father, Mr Benjamin Frank Done, and was the great nephew of the founder, Mr J.W. Done.

Every morning except Sundays for the previous 20 years, foreman baker Mr Harold Spiers, of 15 Amos Lane, starts mixing the dough in the bakery, behind the shop. The white and brown loaves are hand made, not steam baked, which is generally how the large baking combines operate. "I think our method gives the bread more taste and a better texture - it tastes more 'nutty'", commented Mr Spiers.

On average, 200 loaves are baked each day - small, cottage, batch, Vienna and Irish. The Irish loaf is small and rounded and was so named by Mr Spier after he had been on a fishing trip to Ireland and eaten such loaves.

Besides the bread, 30 to 40 dozen cobs and rolls and about 120 cakes and tarts are made to order by Mr Done. It takes him about five hours to ice a three-tier cake.

The Dones' bread won several competitions and diplomas for its quality.

Mrs Elsie Mathews of 123 Waddens Brook Lane worked there so did Lydia Vickers of 5 East Avenue, other assistants were Mrs Audrey Guest of 72 Woden Avenue and Mrs Evelyn Garner of 315 Lichfield Road, also Lizzie Foster with over 58 years service.

Arkinstall's the blacksmiths

Mr Richard Arkinstall was the blacksmiths in Long Knowle Lane. Obviously a blacksmith looks after horses, ie, horse shoes, and other tack that would be needed. It's marvellous to think after the blacksmiths, the premises were used as a garage, and car repairs, another form of transport. Can you remember the name of the people who ran that garage in the early 1960s? There are four houses built on that site now, opposite Sunnydays Premier store, close to the crossroads with the Red Lion.

Hilda Anslow's shop was a wooden hut in Wood End Road, close to the Castle Inn. It sold most things you wanted to buy. She was a large woman, and apparently blind in one eye. I used that shop quite a lot because she was open on Sundays; few opened then in the late 1950s, and early 1960s. Not like today when Sunday is like a normal trading day, in shopping terms that is. The Farm, a former "outdoor" (off licence) used to sell beer and sweets. It was about 100 yards up on the opposite side to Hilda's shop. It is still there today but it is not a shop or an "outdoor". I believe the Mason family used to run that shop. Did they? Just across the road from the "outdoor" were fields. This is a long time ago, but I can remember them. We must be talking about the late 1950s. Did you play in those fields? If so, you will be getting on for at least 50.

6. General events

DENSE fumes and excessive noise from two factories in Well Lane have been the cause of much controversy, angering nearby residents for some years now.

On one Thursday in July of 1962 fumes "fogged out", half of Wednesfield High Street, and people could not stop coughing, the council were going to do something about it, it was in 1962. My! things have not changed much have they?

Born at Wood End

Mr S. Dodd was born at Wood End in 1866, and in 1957 celebrated his 91st birthday.

He started work in the trap trade in 1878 for 3 shillings per week at Roberts, he finished up at Glovers Bros when he was nearly 80. This must have been some sort of record. The Wednesfield branch of the Toc H was founded in 1923, in 1927 the headquarters were in the loft at Staveley House, the police station, it later moved on to a cottage in Taylor Street, and during the War years its headquarters were above the Red Lion in the High Street. It later moved again to land previously a coal wharf in Graisley Lane. This land was given free by Mr Purshouse in 1959. Wednesfield had a wages snatch in 1964. Two men were sentenced at Birmingham Assizes on June 28th, having taken part in a daring wages raid on March 6th.

Wednesfield mourns link with the old days

On October 21st 1965, Wednesfield lost one of its old and best known characters, with the death of Hannah Adey.

Passing of a Grand Old Lady

Mrs Adey was the wife of the late Ben Adey, who was the secretary of the Pyle Lock Sick and Dividend Society for many years. This long established club had the second largest membership in Wednesfield, until 1965, when it ceased to function. Hannah was one of the remaining few old ladies who wore a shawl. And it was a well known fact that the only time she wore a coat was on "Pay Out" nights, once a year, just before Christmas; on these occasions she would assist her husband in this work. Mrs Adey lived for most of her life in a cottage, now demolished, in Rookery Street, a few doors away from that was a fish and chip shop; she could remember the days when a penny purchased a paper full of fish and chips.

In February 1964 Wednesfield's grand old lady Mrs Lewis was 96. She was one of the oldest inhabitants of Wednesfield; her husband Dick Lewis, who died in 1948, was a member of the council for 40 years, he was chairman in 1920.

Mrs Lewis had four sons, most of the land that she farmed, is now built on. Did Mrs Lewis reach the grand old age of 100 and receive a telegram from the Queen?

Wednesfield Police Station

Wednesfield Police Station in Alfred Squire Road was officially opened on 8th October 1971 by Richard C. Sharples Esq. The building contractors were J.F. Wooton of Bloxwich.

Do you recall the old police station that stood on the right hand side? over Rookery Bridge, as though you were going out of Wednesfield, opposite Foulkes coal yard, now selling compost and garden paraphernalia. There used to be another police station up by New Cross, so I have been told.

The police station just over the Rookery Bridge was demolished in the early 1970s.

Libraries

Wednesfield Library opened May 14th 1955, at a cost of over £5,000. The Long Knowle Library opened September 10th 1960.

New shops

Spring 1961 saw some new shops in the village, the newsagents, and chemists, while the private housing estate, just over Gregory's Bridge, steadily progressed. The council offices, The Regal, and Swatmans were no longer the only modern buildings in the centre of Wednesfield.

Hidden behind the crumbling facade of vacated buildings, the Springhill Drapers store took shape, and suddenly, or so it seemed, there it was, one sunny day, open for business, with an opening day give-away of a 10 shilling note for the first dozen customers. I remember standing in the queue from 5.00 am, until they opened.

The rubble filled land on the corner of High Street and Church Street was transformed on March 17th, Deawall opened, followed on the 25th by A.N. Field and Co.

On the other side of the road the M.E.B. had sent out a shoot which grew into the service centre which opened on March 28th.

Girl meets Beatles 1963

"They're Fab!" Miss Janet Boyd of Leveson Road, Ashmore Park was one of the lucky ones to have met the Beatles. Her chance to meet them came, when she won a competition in The Wolverhampton Chronicle. She was led to the dressing rooms in the Gaumont. Here she met the Fab Four, who, in her words were relaxing, listening to their own music on records and drinking coke - repeat coke, not cocaine!

Janet with some other young girls spent 10 minutes talking to them, before coming away with their autographs, she later watched the show and had a lovely time, singing along to some of their songs.

Wednesfield characters

They reckon that if you did not know the name of the Wednesfield tramp, then you do not have much of a memory of Wednesfield. For those who have forgotten, or simply do not know, the name people knew him by was, "Old Herbert". He lived in an old hut on Bacchus End.

I can just about recall him. I was a lad then. Old Herbert used to push a pram round the village. I knew his name, and no doubt many of you can recall him. Mind you, many people were frightened of him.

Halfpenny Harriet was another character you should remember. She would ask for a match, and then want a cigarette to go with it.

Do you remember Leeding? He was the Wednesfield cattle rustler, he stole a cow and painted it white to disguise it. Unfortunately, for him it rained and washed away the paint. He was obviously caught, but I don't know what the law did to him.

The steel bridge over the canal at New Cross junction bears the scars of the ropes that pulled the barges. The horse would walk up the bridge with the barge in tow, the rope that was attached to the animal would rub along the steel hand rail, over the years this has left grooves in the steel. Have you ever noticed? Take a look when you are next at New Cross junction.

Luxury flats opened at Lakefield

A major contribution to Wednesfield housing problems was supposed to come with the opening on August 11th 1962 of the new nine storey block of flats. The new flats were named Grosvenor Court. They were to house 51 families in conditions described at the time as a new note in luxury in the town. Grosvenor Court was later joined by two similar blocks, making accommodation for 153 people, each flat was provided with underfloor heating, a cabinet clothes dryer, and immersion heaters for hot water.

Do you think that the residents of those flats are living in luxury today?

New tenants in multi storey flats

In order to give tenants the best possible chance of settling down quickly in the town's new 20-storey block of flats, William Bentley Court, Mr Patterson, Wednesfield housing manager, gave a short introductory talk for the new tenants, before handing over the keys, in January 1966; although some people had already moved in. With 114 housing units in the block

Fig.30. There is lots of interest in this aerial view. The Police Station, old site across from the council offices, later to be the new market site,

bottom centre. William Bentley Flat, top left, with the market on its and at the back of the Police Station, Wednesfield Social Club. c1974

tenants were encouraged to check with the caretaker if a lift would be available for them at the time they planned to move in. Mr Patterson estimated that the block would be four fifths full by the end of the week.

Some of the tenants who had already moved in were, on the whole, satisfied with their new homes, although there were some complaints about the paint work, the majority were highly enthusiastic about the flats.

A typical comment came from Miss N. Thompson, who moved into Flat 9, "the flat is very nice indeed in every way". Miss Thompson, who formerly lived in Ashmore Park, pointed out that the heating system in the flat was so wonderful, because of the even temperature.

These flats on the Hickman estate were started in 1965. Many Wednesfield people and I believed that it was a mistake. In fact I believe it's the worst decision ever made by the council.

No doubt few councillors living in 1966 had to live in them, because if they had, they would not have been built. As for Miss Thompson's comments in January 1966, she probably got a bit excited about moving into a new home. I have little doubt Miss Thompson's remarks today would be somewhat different.

The sooner these flats are demolished the better, build some decent houses for families. Demolish the flats and rebuild them over Bacchus End; there is plenty of room over there. Do you agree? Or better still what about outer Mongolia?

I bet some of the older inhabitants of Wednesfield can recall the explosion at the Wolverhampton Metal Company on August 21st 1933. It was a huge bang, and could be heard all over Wednesfield. Unfortunately, one person was killed in the explosion. Can you recall Foulkes coal yard, it was where the petrol station stands, just over Rookery Bridge. When we ran out of coal, we used to fetch it from there in an old pram. You could just manage a hundred weight in the pram. Times were hard then. If we had no coal we would burn old shoes to keep us warm. Funny thing is, winters don't seem the same now, as they used to be. Come to think of it neither do the summers.

The Vicarage

The Vicarage, in Vicarage Road. I wonder how many remember the old vicarage was at No. 29, from 1934-1964. It then moved to that of No. 9. I wonder why?

Duke Street premises

Hills fibreglass company on the corner of Duke Street made a number of items out of fibreglass, like fish ponds, canoes, and fireplaces. An old acquaintance of mine, Ray Smith of Wood Avenue used to work there when he was aged 15.

Duke Street was more of a lane, or track, back in the 1950s, and about 50 yards up on the left just inside the field stood two stables, it was a big field, you then came to the allotments which ran alongside the old park.

When I lived in Tithe Road I used to take a short cut across that field where the stables were and it would bring you out at a gate on Gregorys Bridge, just opposite Squires House.

In that field stood a cottage and the people who lived there from 1947 to 1953 were Mr and Mrs Lloyd.

The address for the cottage was 5 The Fields, Lichfield Road, Mr and Mrs Lloyd later moved to Moat Green Avenue. They told me that the rent for that cottage at that time was 7/6d. The estate that is on that land today was built in the late 1950s.

Wednesfield News

Wednesfield's own newspaper, the Wednesfield News, rolled out it first edition in May 1953; the paper being monthly.

It took many months of hard work to produce the first edition, the first six months being regarded as an experimental period, and for that length of time the monthly edition was a limited one.

The main purpose of the paper was to inform the people of Wednesfield what was happening in their own district. Profits from sales would go to the local charities.

The printer of the paper was N. Budd of Temple Street, Wolverhampton, the price was 2d. in 1953; the last edition was number 153 in 1966.

Life savers

In 1965 Robert Rogers aged 15 and Davies Russell aged 14 both rescued a boy from the canal, they received the Royal Humane Society's testimonial, on parchment, from councillor W.H. Bargery, chairman of W.U.D.C.

Orchard Buildings and the Rickyard

The Orchard Buildings was a small compact estate, on open ground near to the Church Bridge, about where the school playground now stands.

The buildings ran right through to what is now called Duke Street; they date back to the middle of the 19th Century.

There were about 37 houses on the estate, one row of houses was called

Lighthouse Row, because this particular row of houses faced the canal facing towards Church Bridge, giving the first lights of Wednesfield to the folk on the barges that were travelling along the dark canal.

The Wyrley and Essington Canal, cut sometime in the late 18th Century had been taken straight through what must have been farmland in this area. A small bridge joined up the land and it was situated about 100 yards from Church Bridge, the name of the bridge, was Barn Bridge. it stood unaltered until it was dismantled in c1967. The Orchard Buildings site was a hive of industry, there were small workshops at the back of the houses, one made locks, another made chains, other small workshops made various things that have long since been forgotten.

You could cross over Barn Bridge to the land behind the Boat Inn, at that time, you could reach the Rickyard where the houses ran from the canal to the road, facing east. Years later Maconkey had a factory by Orchard Buildings, about where the extension has been added to the Church School. On the same site, but over towards the canal, air raid shelters were built during World War Two.

Towards the late 1960s, early 1970s the site was used as a car dismantlers yard.

Council houses

The first council houses built in Wednesfield were those on the Nordley Hill Estate, built between 1921/22, Ashmore Park Estate was a big project taken on by the council, the first houses opened on the estate on Thursday June 16th 1955.

I remember as a young lad playing over Ashmore Park with my brother, Roy, and some of his friends like Fred Homer, Keith Davis, Colin Morris, and Roger Brazier, and others; we used to go bird nesting over there, funny how it's changed over the years.

Fish and chips, and pawnbrokers

Do you recall what stood on the site of The Regal before 1935? Hydes Farm.

Hydes also had the dairy in Bolton Road, the building still stands today.

On the subject of milk, what about Jim Barnes, his depot was in North Street. When I used to help him I was paid half a crown per day - quite something in those days. The batter was delicious at Gradeys fish shop just inside Neachells lane, by the side of the Dog and Partridge. Their fish and chips were out of this world, a bit like those sold in the Black Country Museum, cooked in beef dripping.

Ethel Fisher. I bet this name rings a bell to some older readers. It was a pawnbrokers situated just about where Chris' Delicatessen is today (sorry it is now a fish and chip shop); it was Number 33 back then.

I wonder how many of you actually pawned something there. In those days it was a common occurrence, but today, you don't see many pawnbrokers about, in days gone by it was hard to make ends meet. Mind you, with today's recession it's getting to be the same. Many people would pawn something like the old mans suit, to enable them to have something on the table, when things improved a little, you could go and get the stuff out of hock again.

I wonder if a pawnbroker in the village would have much trade today, what do you think?

St Gregory's

August 1965 saw work start on the new £30,000 Church of St Gregory, in Blackhalve Lane, the building was expected to be completed by August 1966.

Wednesfield weather

Arctic Wednesfield, worst conditions in living memory, and not over yet.

Those were the headlines in the Wednesfield News. When the cold spell began, towards the end of December 1962, few people can have had any idea of the havoc that was to come.

Difficulties were apparent within a week, but serious troubles did not develop until early January, then as snow and ice took a firmer grip on roads, and drives. The collection of refuse from houses in the district became disorganised, and overflowing dustbins bore eloquent evidence to the narrow margin, on which our services operate. Taking into consideration the atrocious conditions, the collection crews did well, the way they handled their vehicles.

The bad weather did not let up until towards the end of February 1963. I can remember this bad weather; certainly the worst in my experience.

There was another bit of bad weather in Wednesfield, but it's unlikely any readers would have been affected by it. In April 1903 Wednesfield was struck by a hail storm. The hail was said to have been as big as tennis balls, as reported in The Express & Star.

You could not imagine the damage a storm like that can do, not only to property, but to anyone caught in it; it would have been no use putting up an umbrella. You would not have known what to do, which way to run.

Gwynn Morgan Hall

The Gwynn Morgan Hall opened in March 1957 by Clarence Haden; it was named after the late clerk of the council.

Wednesfield Market off to a flyer

After some delay - unavoidable, but none the less, frustrating - Tuesday, 13th December 1960 saw the long-awaited market open. The orderly rows of little stalls, with their gaily stripped awnings, lent an air of bright cheerfulness to the atmosphere of Christmas. The car park was across the road from The Regal in Alfred Squire Road. Some of the traders at the time were F. Bonser & Son, hardware glass and china, Hilda Peach, curtains and dress materials, Birch's footwear, O.J. Edwards, high class butcher, O. Downes, fruit and veg, Holyhead soap powders and detergent, W.H. Jervis, poultry eggs and farm produce, and many more. In the 1970s the market moved site, to land by the council offices; I don't think that it helped much. A market can only succeed with the support of the local people and at the moment that support is dwindling. I traded there for 12 months, and found it difficult.

People complained that there was no selection on the market, saying that at one time there were seven stalls selling baby clothes, and that the quality of the goods had fallen off. A firmer stance should have been taken about how many of the same products allowed to be sold. I have found that the quality of the goods sold has always been good. People should use the market more often, because if they don't, well... we will lose it: It's as simple as that! The market has moved yet again, this time to the High Street. This can only be good for it; let's hope that the market can get back to how it used to be in the early '60s.

Wednesfield did have a market during the War years, it used to be by the side of the Pyle Cock, it was called the Toffee market, Steve Hargreaves ran it, it did quite well on its one day per week trading.

Coronation street parties

Many streets in Wednesfield held Coronation day street parties. Mattox Road held theirs on the Monday of June 1st 1953 at 3.00pm, each child received a mug filled will sweets, the streets were floodlit after dark and dancing took place in Mattox Road, all the good work had been done by, Butler, Long, Essex, Newton, Turner, White, and Rose.

Mr and Mrs Hadley and staff of the "Cross Guns", held a party for the customers on the day, and also held a party for the children on the following Saturday.

The customers of the "Castle" made a grand effort to give some 130 children a party, which was held at the Castle Inn, by kind permission of Mr S. Hargreave, the licensee, on Saturday, May 30th. The committee, which consisted of Rumford, Hancock, Buckley, Parker and Mr F Peplow, left no stone unturned in their efforts to give the children a good time.

I bet a good time was had by all at these parties. I dare say some people would be going backwards and forwards to the different streets and pubs holding parties.

Nearly 8,000 people attended a Coronation Carnival on King George V Playing Fields on Saturday July 4th 1953. The photograph shows ladies from East Avenue, congregating in the tea tent. By the look of them, they were all enjoying themselves, even though it was raining outside. I wonder which tent the men occupied? The baby show was won by M. Fucico/ R. Fellows.

The following chapter was taken from the Wednesfield News, the report is on the Coronation day celebrations, Coronation day, 2nd June 1953.

'The council decided that although it is appreciated that some families will wish to celebrate the occasion by looking or listening to the T.V. or Radio programmes for most of the day, it was considered that Coronation day being a public holiday, would be the day found to be most convenient for people generally to come together to be entertained, it was therefore agreed to concentrate on Coronation day, and to commence the proceedings on King George V Playing Fields at approx. 2.30pm, when much of the Coronation service will be over.

'An ambitious programme of entertainments of all descriptions had been arranged and this will go on until well after dark. Several marquees had been hired and in one of these, concerts will be given by the Wolverhampton girls choir, the Masquerades television show, Mr J Leighton's concert party, the Wednesfield Male Voice Choir, Mr W. Alan King and others.

'For the children, Punch and Judy Shows would be given, there will also be dancing on the green.

'After dusk there will be fireworks, and a bonfire.

'Refreshments, including intoxicants, will be available on the park, and the council will entertain the old people to tea, they will also each be provided with a quarter pound of tea.

'Each child in the district will be provided with a pencil box containing chocolates, and the council are making a grant of one shilling per pupil, to each school in the district for the entertainment of their scholars.

'There will also be a competition for the best decorated street in the district, the judging to take place during Coronation week.

'On Coronation day despite grey clouds and almost continuous rain, packed audiences attended the concerts organised by the council, in a

Fig.31.I often swam in this paddling pool, opened 1939 in the bottom of Wednesfield Playing Field park. Did you? The lad, bottom left, seems familiar. Is he any relation of yours?

marquee, on the playing fields, the artists all proved to be of very high order, and the programme was greatly appreciated.

'The compares at the afternoon performances were councillors Broomhall, and Higgs, and at the evening performance councillors, Haden, and Ratcliffe.

'The council had invited all old people of the district as well as disabled ex servicemen to tea, and despite the rain some 300 accepted the invitation.

'Prizes given by the council for the best decorated street were won by:-

1st Woden Avenue, 2nd Lawrence Avenue, and 3rd Bolton Road.

'The final of the Bowling competition held on Thursday the 4th June was won by Mr George Howells, with Mr H. Done as runner up, vouchers were presented to them and to other semi finalists, Mr A Moreby, and Mr H. Warner, by the chairman of the council.

Prizes for the best dressed shop windows were won as follows.

Class for shops selling things to use:-

1st Mr J.A. Thompson, 8 High Street

2nd Mr P. Tedstill, 3 Rookery Street

3rd Mr C. Squires Hardware Ltd, Rookery Street

Class for shops selling things to wear:-

1st Miss Norton, 66-68 Rookery Street

2nd Mrs Broomhall, 30 High Street

Fig.32. Ladies from East Avenue congregate in the tea tent at King George Playing Fields, Coronation day carnival, Saturday July 3rd 1953. There was presumably another tent for the men.

3rd Mrs Edwards, 62 New Street
Class for shops selling things to eat:-
1st M/s J.H. Sambrook, butchers, 75 Lichfield Road
2nd Tie between M/s Jurdison, fruiterers, 30 Nordley Road and Mr H.G. Beech, Wood End
3rd also a tie between Mr H.A. Smith, 1 Lawfred Avenue, and Mrs H.E. Sambrook, Hadleys Fold, Neachells Lane.'

I wonder if that was the fish and chip shop just around the corner from the Dog and Partridge.

There was also a special recommendation for Mrs I. Holmes coffee shop, Well Lane.

Did you get one of those pencil boxes? Can you remember going to Wednesfield King Geroge's Field on Coronation day? Can you recall any of the shops that won prizes?

A great time was had by all, and it just goes to show that Wednesfield can unite, and get together to celebrate a great occasion like the Coronation. The prizes were given at a function at Swatmans Cafe on Wednesday 17th June.

On the same day 338 old age pensioners attended a special showing of the colour film "Elizabeth is Queen" at The Regal cinema, the show was free, and everyone was highly delighted with the film of the Coronation.

Wednesfield Carnivals

What's happened to the Wednesfield Carnivals? It's been a while since we had the sort of carnival Wednesfield was once renowned for.

I suppose it's all down to money. Shops and factories that used to sponsor it are no longer interested. Carnivals of the recent past are just a remnant of those from long ago.

Some remember the marquees in King George's Playing Fields, one for the beer, one for the tea and cakes, and one for the band, a cow roasting on a spit, army displays, five a side football, whippet racing, and many more attractions. Wednesfield should have those good old carnivals again; after all

Fig.33. A Wednesfield carnival float, owned by Grosvenor. Coal merchant Mary Bodley is second from the right, she supplied the photograph.

Willenhall can still manage theirs.

One of the carnivals we had in 1955 attracted a staggering 20,000 people. Yes, I'll say it again - 20,000 people!

The 1956 carnival saw one of the most interesting capers with the "needle in a haystack" competition, or was it a treasure hunt? Carnival chief Mr Norman Pursehouse forked the hay packs with great energy to scatter straw over the mysterious envelope containing ten shillings: Wow! that was money then! Sixty yards away half of Wednesfield's juvenile population watched with glaring eyes where he placed the envelope. When the Carnival Queen, Patricia Tasker, dropped her handkerchief for the hunt to start, a stampede took place that made the Klondike gold rush look like a walk in the park.

Someone found the envelope, but who? I'll give you ten bob if you tell me who found it... the rotters... I was in that stampede. Trying to find out who found it... well, it's like looking for a needle in a haystack!

Wednesfield welcomes the Queen

Cheering crowds line streets on Town's great day. A gaily decorated Alfred Squire Road, including a wonderful display of flowers in front of the council offices, welcomed the Queen on her short walk in Wednesfield during her journey from Wolverhampton to Walsall.

Her Majesty, smiling, in the sunshine and wearing a beige coat with hat to match, stepped out of the Royal car on to the carpet, and walked to the red canopy erected in front of the entrance to the council offices. There she was met by a number of councillors, amongst whom were the new chairman of the council, H.P. Fitzmaurice and his wife.

When the Queen stepped forward to sign the visitors books for Wednesfield and Willenhall she picked up the pen and remarked "Will it write?".

The Queen signed the books and was then handed a composure and presented with pink roses and white lilies by petite, Carol Burns, aged seven, of 29 Pickering Road. The Queen spent a little time talking to councillors and members of the public, before she made her way in the Royal car down Lakefield Road where she was welcomed by tremendous cheering from some 6,000 schoolchildren waving to the Queen as she went by, we all had small flags to wave and it seemed like we stood for hours, before we caught a glimpse of her passing by. Come to think of it, it was a couple of hours - still, it was worth it.

Prior to the Queen coming to Wednesfield, a ballot was held at all Wednesfield primary schools, to decided upon the girl who would present the Queen with a bouquet on her visit. The eventual winner was Linda

Helena Wytha. Another name drawn was Carol Burns, the reserve. Something must have happened for Carol presented the flowers to the Queen, perhaps Linda was unwell.

The Queen's visit, on 24th May 1962, is one of the most special days in the annuals of Wednesfield; it must have been a great day for Carol, also.

7. Sport

King George's Field

KING GEORGE V had deeply at heart the welfare of the rising population, and no happier or more beneficent means of perpetuating his memory could be devised than to provide throughout the length and breadth of the land, recreation grounds, to be known as King George's Fields.

The project had much to commend it, the need for open spaces, to which young people and children could go for exercise, and games, safe from the perils of the streets. The scheme was a flexible one and could be carried out in each locality, according to its requirements, it enlisted local interest and support, it was helped by gifts of land, as well as money, each field would have a distinctive gateway of a uniform type, or other appropriate visible commemoration of his late Majesty, who died on 30th January 1936.

It was on the 3rd November 1936, that King George's Fields Foundation was constituted by Trust Deed.

Wednesfield's King George Field was opened in 1939, at a capital cost of £8,500, of which a grant of £1,000 was given by the Foundation; the area covered 13.79 acres.

The photograph shows the children splashing, and playing in the paddling pool on the opening day 1939.

At a guess, those kids in the photograph are now aged about 80. Are you there? Try as I have, I cannot trace any of the children shown.

The old park, or flower park was laid down in 1925/6. It used to have a lily pond, round which people use to sit.

Wednesfield soccer stars - Past and present

Wednesfield soccer followers who watched the career of Dick Taylor, kept their fingers crossed for him in his efforts to sign a star winger, which, we hope, together with his coaching skills, will bring Aston Villa the success that will take the "acting", from his present appointment, and Dick a long contract as manager of his famous club.

In these seasons of declining gates and increasing wages of players, the life of a football manager can be so insecure, but Dick did well to win the central league last season.

Dick seems most able to cope with the job, and with the directors prepared to give him a chance, it only remains for the supporters to "play fair", for a time.

The Villa Park crowd are known to be reasonable, not having been greatly spoiled over the last 30 years, as at Molineux, and if they give him the support he deserves "great days" should be on the way again for the claret and blue. Dick whose career has taken him to Grimsby and Scunthorpe as a player, and Sheffield United, and Aston Villa as Assistant manager to Joe Mercer, went from schoolboy football to Grimsby Town with a Wednesfield friend, Jack Trench of Victoria Road, who was later domiciled in Grimsby as a member of the police force.

Hoping, too, for Villa greatness, and all that it brings is Wednesfield's John Sleeuwenhoek, Villa's talented centre half who must be on the verge of international honours. With John now in possession of the centre half position, and with another local "John" Morby, having successfully held it in opposition to such greats as Tommy Lawton before unfortunate cartilage trouble curtailed his career, Wednesfield has certainly claimed an interest in Villa Park affairs. Sadly, I have to write that John Sleeuwenhoek, very well known and liked in Wednesfield, died in 1989.

John Sleeuwenhoek

The old post office that stood in the High Street, later turned into a newsagents, this was run by Jack Needham, the old Wolves inside forward who signed professional forms for Nottingham Forest when he was 18 in 1904, and on transfer played for the Wolves, who were then in the Second Division. Jack kept the newsagents for four years, later it became known as J.A. Thompsons newsagents, address being 8 High Street.

Another professional footballer from Wednesfield was Alec Johnson, he played for a host of clubs, he also did some scouting for Wolves and Manchester United, he also had links with Crewe Alexander. Alec lives on the Cannock Road by Westcroft, he has run kids teams at St Chad's School for a number of years. He is a good friend, and what he doesn't know about football, well... it's not worth knowing. Dave Wilson of Graisley Lane, was another pro footballer.

Wednesfield Football Club was founded in 1946, chiefly as a result of requests from returned service men. Since its inception the club has had many successes, and fully deserves the continued support of those interested in its activities.

The pitch was at one time on King George Playing Fields with the headquarters on a small piece of land in North Avenue, by the allotments, it was later renamed Wednesfield Town Football Club.

There are some photographs of the Church School inter football team 1955/6 in the old school playground (see pages 122 and 133). Mr Whelan to the right, Fred Snape, Dennis Harris, Bill Rushton and of the Howes sons. Do you know anyone else in the photograph? Also the 1947/48 Church School Football Team with Jack Morby to the right of the picture.

Boxing

Wednesfield has its own boxing champion in the dynamic form of Steve Saville, also known as the Wednesfield Bomber.

Steve boxes at lightweight. His fight record reads won 21, with 9 of those being KOs, he has only lost four fights. He is the Midland Lightweight Champion, the sole reigning Midland title holder from the Black Country. Steve's next fight is due to take place on September 18th for the English Lightweight championship at Wolverhampton Civic Hall. He certainly deserves a crack at this title, best of

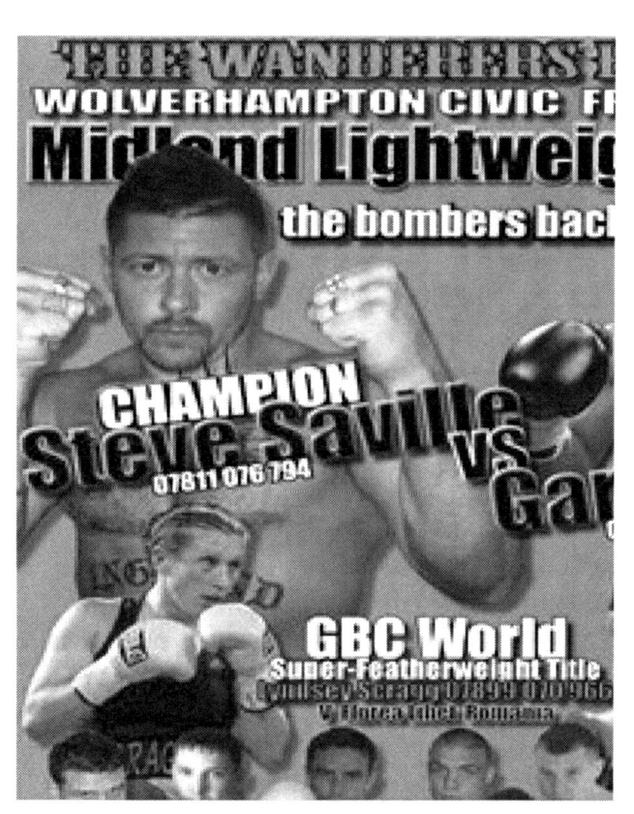

Steve Saville

luck, Steve. I am sure all Wednesfield are behind you in your bid to be the champ.

Johnny Prescott

The British Heavyweight Champion trained here. Will Wednesfield be able to claim this distinction after 15th June 1965.

Johnny Prescott, challenger for Henry Cooper's heavyweight boxing crown, is to use Wednesfield Amateur Boxing Club's gym, at the Cottage Homes as his training quarters for his title fight to be held at St Andrew's Ground in Birmingham, arranged by Mr Alex Griffiths.

Those were the headlines in the local Wednesfield News over 30 years ago. Perhaps you can recall the winner. Did Wednesfield claim the headlines after all?

Well, the fight did not take place on the 15th of June because it poured with rain all day, and the fight had to be postponed until the Thursday evening of the 17th. No. Wednesfield could not claim those headlines, because George Biddles, Prescott's manager told the ref to stop the fight, this was in the tenth round - My boy has taken enough punishment, he said.

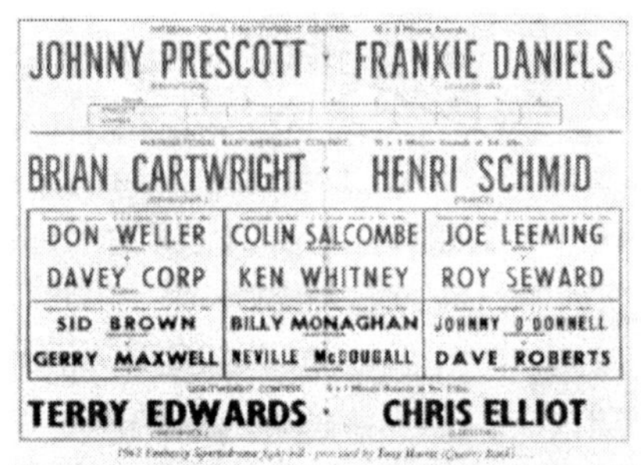

Johnny Prescott

George Griffiths

Laura Blyth writes in *The Express & Star* this year, 2009:-

'The West Midlands boxing world is in mourning for George Griffiths.

'The long-serving president of Wolverhampton Amateur Boxing, who has died aged 86, had been a fighter, referee and

George Griffiths

Figure. 66. George Griffiths in later life.

matchmaker during his career.

'George, who was also a top amateur cyclist, died on June 23 after suffering from heart problems.

'His son, Nick, a current director at the club, said his father would be sadly missed by everyone at Wolverhampton ABC. "Boxing was my dad's life," he said. "He fought in the armed forces and then trained boxers in Wolverhampton and also became a referee."

'George, of Mill Lane, Wednesfield, who went to Lichfield Road Infants in Wednesfield, which is now Edward The Elder Primary & Nursery School, started boxing at the age of 11 and reached his peak in the 1930s and 1940s.

'He then joined the armed forces and served as a lance sergeant in the North Staffordshire Regiment, stationed in Shetland. While there, he took part in boxing contests, winning several military cups for his efforts. He was then posted to Juno beach in France along with Canadian troops during the Normandy D-Day landings, suffering a blast injury before he was discharged.

'Nick, who is also the community officer at Kidderminster Harriers, continued: "He joined Wolverhampton ABC as a matchmaker in the 1950s.

'"He also became a referee and did that for about 30 years until 1978.

'"Interestingly, he was one of the last to referee outside the ring which is different to how it's done today." George will also be missed by the older generation of the club who knew him very well.

'"He retired from active involvement at the club in 1978 but continued to serve as the president," said Nick, who explained how his father also enjoyed football and cycling.

'George's wife Audrey died 15 years ago. She had owned the fancy dress shop Audrey's in Wood End, Wednesfield.'

'Griffiths, a self-employed, plumber for most of his life, left behind Nick 45, daughter Toni 34, and two grandchildren.'

May the memory of George, whose funeral was held at West Chapel, Bushbury Crematorium, be long in the hearts of Wednesfield folk.

Bert Adey

Who in this district, or indeed in many parts of the West Midlands has not heard of Bert Adey.

Sportsman and popular licensee of the Pear Tree. At the end of World War One, when making his name as a boxer, Bert, had ambitions to become a licensee, and during training runs, he often passed the old Pear Tree, then a semi-country house of a very different character to the present large modern premises.

Mr. A. Adey

Being a shrewd man, he visualised it in years to come, and made a mental note, that this was the house he would like. Meanwhile, he proceeded with his boxing career, with no small measure of success, and became a professional, winning many fights.

His life as a licensee began in 1921, at the Locomotion, Stafford Road, Wolverhampton.

After four years there he moved on to the Yew Tree, Poole Street, Wolverhampton. Here he remained for six years. By this time, 1931, Wolverhampton was expanding rapidly. Council houses were creeping towards the Pear Treet and Bert Adey, making a successful application for this house, realised his early ambition.

Bert moved into the house, but it was not easy-going, in fact he struggled on during this slump period and he realised that he had to do something to attract trade. One of his early efforts was to purchase a donkey, which he kept in the garden at the rear of the pub.

Children being what they are, soon persuaded their parents that the Pear Tree was the place to drink on a summers day. The children made such good use of the donkey rides that two more had to be added to satisfy the demand.

TOMMY ROGERS

Born at Portobello in 1913, Tommy Rogers already had ten consecutive wins 'under his belt' when he fought his first ten-rounder, at Dudley on March 18th. 1931 (his 18th. birthday) and gained a points decision over Bill Billington. From then on his career really took off as promoters vied for his 'crowd-pulling' style. His best years were undoubtedly 1931-1933. During this period he took part in 51 contests - winning 39,

Bert also promoted boxing contests in an adjoining field. He took advantage of his former career and became a promoter. One of his most successful ventures in this direction was on an August Bank Holiday Monday in 1933, when he promoted the Southern Area Featherweight Championship between Tommy Rogers of Portobello, Willenhall, and Tommy Hyams of London. The fight attracted some three thousand people. Tommy Rogers won in the fifth round.

In 1937 the present Pear Tree was built and was surrounded by many houses.

Bert moved in from the old establishment and became the proud licensee of a modern house, where he was ably assisted by Mrs Adey, daughter Pat, and a loyal staff. At this point mention must be made of Pat Adey whose help and co-operation made it possible for me to write this piece. Thank you, Pat.

Bert had many arguments with Wednesfield council. Just one of these was in a letter from the council to him, dated 1st April 1933. The letter goes as follows:-

'Dear Sir,

At a meeting of the council held last night, your proposal to hold a boxing exhibition on Sunday next was unanimously deplored. It was felt that such an exhibition was most undesirable and

Fig.44. The Southern Area Feather Weight Championship on Bank Holiday Monday, 1933 between Tommy Rogers (Portobello) and Tommy Hyams of London. Over 3,000 spectators watched Tommy Rogers win the 5th round.

```
would be against the wishes of an overwhelming ma-
jority of the people of Wednesfield.
 In these circumstances, I am instructed to re-
quest that the arrangements for the exhibition be
cancelled at once. I think it only right to call
your attention to the Sunday Observance Act 1780,
under which you render yourself liable to a penal-
ty of £100, should you proceed with the promotion
of the exhibition as advertised in the press. '
```

Bert ignored the council and put on fights at the Pear Tree, attracting thousands of people, proving that the council were wrong in saying that Wednesfield people did not want these boxing matches on Sundays.

If you look at what takes place on Sundays now, it shows how out of date the council were; but more importantly how forward thinking Bert Adey was.

Bert stood up for what he thought was right. He continued successfully to run the Pear Tree until 1959. Sadly, he in no longer with us. I am sure many people will remember his name; a great man.

Horse racing

Frank Morby of Well Lane - Wednesfield jockey - reached his 20th birthday on 12th April 1954. He had been apprenticed to the stables of G. Colling at Newmarket for five years, although still apprentice he won five races, one of these being an important one at Leicester, beating Sir Gordon Richards, and several other prominent jockeys, Frank will remember that win all his life, as Gordon Richards was knighted on the same day. Frank was an all-round sportsman, being the champion runner at Newmarket for two years running. Another day Frank will remember was when he was thrown from his horse at Royal Ascot in front of the Queen, fortunately he was not hurt. Frank, your pictures hung in Wednesfield Social Club for years. I wonder where they are now.

Pigeons

One of the principal pastimes of local inhabitants of yesteryear, and indeed still is by quite a few, was pigeon racing. Pigeons were mostly divided into two classes, long distance, and half miles.

Most of the pubs round Wednesfield staged their challenge, and counter challenges. One such challenge was that by old Sam Potts, he was urged by his pals to challenge Tom Bishop to a race, to start from Tut Park (an old name for some cornfields near to the existing Nordley Hill) and to finish at their respective pens, two pigeons a side. Tom Bishop's pals, somehow obtained access to Sam Potts pigeons the evening before the race. They sorted out two long distance pigeons and placed them in a basket which Potts used for carrying his birds. Sam Potts' pals on the other hand, got at Bishops' pigeons and clipped the wings of two of his half miles, also placing them in his basket.

When the race took place, Bishops' pigeons of course were unable to fly and had to foot slog, driven along by Bishops pals, Potts birds being long distance flew for miles and were hours before returning, so that the birds that walked won the race. I don't know about that do you?

Another well known family for keeping pigeons was the Marstons.

8. World Wars, theatres and cinemas

HOW many people of Wednesfield actually take the time to really look at things in their own backyard.

You tend to take the buildings and roads for granted, if you really take time and look you will find things that you did not realise were there. Take the church for example. Take a walk round it; it's free you know.

Take time out, one day, and you will see a different side to the hustle and bustle of present day life in Wednesfield. Try relaxing in the garden of remembrance at the side of the Library, while there have a sit down and think. Then have a read of the stone memorial which was put up to commemorate the brave men of Wednesfield who laid down their lives in the Great Wars.

'In grateful memory to the men of Wednesfield who laid down their lives in the Great War 1914-1918'

J. ALLEN	J. BANKS	W.T. CHAPMAN
C. ANSLOW	J. BANKS	F. COLLINS
G. ANSLOW	S. BARNES	P. CONWAY
S. ARIS	J. BELLINGHAM	W. CONWAY
D. BALL	F. BRADLEY	A. COOPER
A. BANKS	W. BURGESS	J. CRAVEN
G. BANKS	J. BUTLER	F. CROCKETT
J. BANKS	G. CALDWELL	S. DAVIES
J. BANKS	J.H. CASEY	A.C. DAY
J. BANKS	W. CASWELL	E.S. DODD

J.R. DODD
E. EGGLINGTON
W.A. FELLOWS
B. FREEMAN
T. FROGGATT
R.T. GRAYSON
J.T. GREGORY
A. GRIFFITHS
W. GRIFFITHS
C. GULLEY
H.F. GULLEY
J.W. HADLEY
J. HANCOX
R. HARRIS
H. HARTILL
T. HARTILL
E. HILL
S. HILL
J.H. HINDLEY
S. HORTON
W.C. HORTON
G. HUMPHREYS
E. JACKSON
C. JENKINS
A. JONES
C.P. JONES
J. KIRK
S. KIRK
A.W. LATHE
J. LEE
A.H. LEWIS
R. LEWIS
A.E. LLOYD
W. LLOYD
S. MANNION
B. MATTOX
F. MATTOX
A. McCONKEY
W.C. MILES
F. MILLENCAMP
W.H. MILLS
B.W. MINCHER
A. MORETON
C. MORGAN
W. MORGAN
J.P.MORRIS
T. MORRIS
A. NICHOLLS
H.R.PHILLIPS
W.A. PHILLIPS
J.M. POWELL
F. PRITCHARD
S. PUGH
T. REYNOLDS
J. SMALLMAN
W. SMALLMAN
N.F. SMITH
W.A. STANIFSTREET
W.S. SUTTON
A.E. SWEETING
W.H. TAYLOR
N. TEAGUE
C.A. THOMPSON
C.H. TOMLINSON
A. TONKINSON
C. TURNER
H. WALKER
J.G. WAPPLES
F. WARREN
H. WASHBROOK
J. WATTS
J.E. WATTS
R. WATTS
G. WEDGE
A.W. WHITEHOUSE
E. WHITEHOUSE
F.W. WHITEHOUSE
G.E. WILLIAMS
J.J. WILLIAMS
W. WILLIAMS
T. WILTSHIRE

For Second World War, 1939-1945, we remember.

I.J.ADEY
F. BANKS
T.W. BANKS
S. BELLINGHAM
G.F. BISHOP
H. BOWEN
J. BUTLER
R. CADMAN
P.R. CARTWRIGHT
A. CASEY
W.F. COOPER
E.J. COX
J. CRAVEN
G.A. DAVIS
J.A. DAVIES
J.H. DAVIES
E.R. EVANS
H. EVANS
F.C. FOSTER
R.A. FRY
C. GILES
G.C. GREEN
L. GUEST
C. HAZLEWOOD

D.E. HUGHES
G. JENKINS
R.G. JERVIS
T. JEYNES
W. JOHNSON
R. JONES
J.H. LOVATT
G. LYONS
V. MARTIN
R. MEANS
G. MOLINEAUX
J. MORRIS
J.F.K. MORRIS
A. PEDLEY
C.H. PURSEHOUSE
K. REDDISH
F.A. REYNOLDS
E.W. ROBERTS
J. ROWLEY
T. ROWLEY
J.E. ROWLEY
J.T. ROUND
H. RUSSELL
A.G. SALT
C. SIMPSON
G.L. SKIDMORE
R. SPENCER
K. VINCENT
C. WALLBANK
J. WATERHOUSE
G. WEIR
A. WOOLLEY

The following words spoken by Winston Churchill are most appropriate:-

Dedicated to the few and to the many who helped make victory possible'.
Battle of Britain August 8th to September 15th 1940.

'Never in the field of human conflict was so much owed by so many to so few.'
Winston Churchill, House of Commons, 20th August 1940.

There are some well-known names on the stone. No doubt many people will remember them. You can often find flowers placed in front of it.

The Garden of Remembrance was officially opened on Sunday November 8th 1959.

Times were hard for those on the "Home Front" too. Many women were working in factories to help meet the demand for vital parts needed towards the war effort.

Wartime interlude

During the war years, 1939-1945, Sunday concerts were put on for local troops, and for many war charities. Many famous stars and bands have been on the stage at these concerts, and they were all well patronised. But it became very difficult to get transport for these artists and bands, due to the fact that petrol was only allowed for special work, so they were stopped.

The local troops, however, made an application for Sunday film shows, and after a stormy debate by the local council of the day, it was agreed to apply for Sunday opening. This was granted and remained so.

Alex Tuck was manager at The Regal. He had come from the Dunstall cinema. He stayed three years, and then moved to the cinema at Fallings Park.

Mr H. J. E. Davies was the manager from September 1938, and stayed for the duration. Many of you will recall Albert Brookes, the commissionaire. He had a personality all of his own, he was a nice man. He kept out any unwanted troublemakers.

The Regal Cinema had seats for 1,028. It closed on March 17 1962, a sad day in Wednesfield's history. I believe Alec Davis was caretaker whilst The Regal was being dismantled.

How could the council let The Regal close?? They said, it was in the name of progress: a silly, stupid excuse.

The Regal provided Wednesfield inhabitants with entertainment on their own doorstep. Here is a programme of what was shown at the Regal in 1955. Thursday, March 10th for three days:-

Robert Donat, and Kay Walsh in 'Lease of Life' (U) in Eastmancolour.

Underwater frills in 'Hunters of

Fig.34. (Left). The Regal Cinema, 1957. If you look closely you can see the flower bed just the other side of those two people. I am sure that the flowers were tulips. To the right is the old Wesleyan Chapel.

Fig.35. (Below). Some of The Regal Cinema's staff. Mr Brookes is to the left, and I believe that could be Mr Davies next to him. They wore great uniforms. I liked the gloves.

the Deep' (U).

Thursday. March 31st for three days:- Alfred Hitchcock's latest thriller, 'Rear Window' (A) in Technicolour, starring James Stewart, and Grace Kelly.

Saturday mornings were for kids. There were stars like Buster, Crabbe,

Figures. 37. (Above) The Smack Cinema. (Bottom). This was the rear of The 'Smack', once used as an entrance on the canal side. The picture was taken prior to the fire of 1990; the building was demolished and rebuilt.

Laurel and Hardy, and the Artemus Boys. Yes, those were the Saturdays I used to look forward to.

The Regal Cinema

The Regal Cinema has given pleasure to many thousands of people in and around Wednesfield for many years.

The opening night was October 14th 1935. Prices of admission were 6d., 9d and 1/. 'Reprieved' and 'Bulldog Jack (aka Alias Bulldog Drummond)' (1935) were the films that were shown on that evening.

The Regal was built for the late Sir S.W. Clift, and Leon Salberg, both of whom were well known in the cinema industry.

It was the first of a circuit to be known as the Clifton Cinemas.

The Regal enjoyed steady patronage right up to the outbreak of the Second World War. As far as records show, it seems that Wednesfield had not got used to its new cinema, and the habit of going to town (Wolverhampton) to the cinema was something, that could not be broken. With the outbreak of war, the black out and lack of transport, Wednesfield's Regal came into its own, and residents found they could get the same entertainment at their local cinema, at lower prices, than they could at a town centre cinema.

The Smack/ Ideal Cinema

The other cinema in the village was the Ideal Cinema, or more commonly known as the Smack. It was so called because there were lots of flees in the building, and whilst watching a film, it was very common to hear a smack as people went to whack the flee against their legs or bodies. The Smack was originally built as a chapel in 1852. It did not become a cinema until c1912. The entrance was from the canal side. There was seating for around 350 people, and the last film shown was in c1957.

The building was a carpet warehouse until a fire burnt it out on Sunday evening 11th November 1990. This photograph dates from before the fire. According to *The Express & Star* the fire was started by arsonists. It was not clear how the attackers gained entry.

Rookery Street was closed from 10.35pm until 9.00am the following morning, after fears that parts of the structure could collapse.

Hall Street Tivoli Theatre

This was nicknamed the Old Smack. It still stands today, in Hall Street. It began life as a Salvation Army Temperance Hall in about 1860. It later became a place of entertainment and gaiety.

I wonder how much longer the building will be left standing with all the redevelopment going on round it.

Regular visitors to the Smack/ Ideal Cinema would remember the properties that stood next door, some yards off the main road and overlooking at the rear the Wyrley and Essington Canal, No. 1 Rookery Street stood majestically for some 120 years as one of the first blocks of Wednesfield property built during the Industrial Revolution.

Covering approximately three quarters of an acre, the area contained 14 two storey terraced type houses, and 33 people shared W.C., water, and other services, which were all located 8-20 yards from the houses.

The last of these houses were demolished in December 1955, and with demolition completed, 1958, saw the erection of a petrol and repair garage, to meet the ever growing traffic, traversing the main road to Wolverhampton.

The scene has faded but for its occupants, some of whom may be alive today. The memory lingers on. Drying their washing on different days in an open courtyard, hasty trips to shared facilities, and waiting behind their neighbour whilst she filled her kettle, before they too could make their morning brew. The complications of bath night, those steep dark stairs; memories are made of these things.

Fig. 38. Tivoli Theatre, Hall Street. It is now incorporated into Hill Bros. builders' yard.

The Lancaster Bomber crash

One story that most Wednesfield got wrong was the Lancaster Bomber crash on the Lichfield Road, or could it have been a Halifax Bomber?

The following is a report that appeared in The Express & Star on Friday, May 18th 1945.

Seven killed in Lancaster Bomber crash on road at Wednesfield

by our special correspondent

Seven members of the crew of a four engined Lancaster Bomber were killed last night when the machine crashed in Lichfield Road, Wednesfield, and was blown to pieces. Four bricklayers who were on the road some distance away were thrown to the ground by the blast and had to be treated for shock.

Pieces of the bomber were strewn over an area of two miles wide. There was not a single piece of the plane left larger than a table top.

The bomber came from East Kirkby, Lincolnshire, and was on a routine training flight.

When I arrived at the scene shortly after the crash, firemen were playing on the wreckage and had the fire well under control.

A long stretch of hedge had been burnt to the ground, and the grass of a field scorched and burned over a large area.

Big crater

There were no signs of the engines, but the crash caused a crater five feet deep in the road, and it is quite likely that they were buried.

The chimney pot of Moat House Farm was thought to be knocked off by the bomber, and this was the only damage to houses, of which there are plenty 200 yards towards the centre of Wednesfield.

Traffic between Wednesfield and Bloxwich had to be diverted, and the road is still unpassable today.

Joe Castree, an Express & Star transport driver, who was one of the first on the scene, told me that he was handing a parcel of newspapers to a girl in Stubby Lane when he heard the plane flying very low.

It passed right over me he said, and there seemed to be two explosions in the air before the crash.

Couldn't do anything

I ran to the spot immediately, but it was impossible for me to do anything, as there was just a lot of wreckage scattered over a wide area, and no signs of any member of the crew except fragmentary remains. Bullets were exploding, and flares were going off. Another witness told me that the bullets went off like a firework display, as many of them appeared to be tracers. The plane seemed to come down in a swift vertical dive, he added.

An R.A.F. inquiry will be held.

The date of the crash was Thursday 17th May 1945 at approximately 5.15pm, there were seven crew members. The only remaining question is, from which direction did the plane come from. Some people say it came from Wednesfield Park, and that it actually tried to land there but there were too many children playing there, as stated by Terry Morgan of Tithe Road, this would correspond with the pot being knocked off Moat House Farm, but would that agree with going over Stubby Lane. I am not so sure. Do you agree?

The Lancaster in the photograph was a MK1 PP687, built by Vickers Armstrong in early 1945. It served with No. 149 Squadron from March 26th 1945, and No. 44 Squadron from October 9th 1945.

Fig. 45b. The Avro Lancaster. Due to its outstanding efficiency and performance the Lancaster was able to attack heavily defended strategic targets deep in enemy territory with a heavier bomb load than any other World War Two aircraft. It has a-wing span of 102'; a length of 69' 6", and a maximum speed of 275 mph.

9. Work

The Monkey Muck works

THE MONKEY Muck works, this was the manure works just off Rookery, to the rear of the New Inns public house. It was called Monkey Muck works because of the bad smell it gave off.

The building no longer stands today, but I was lucky to have the opportunity to take a photograph of it prior to its demolition in the early 1990s.

In the photograph, the building carries the name of W.L.G. Sidebothams, and Joseph Collins & Sons, later occupants of the building when it was an engineering workshop.

The true age of the building is not clear, but it is well over 120 years old, being shown on a local map of 1886, where it is described as Manure and Acid Works. Sidebothams had another building close by, clearly shown on the photograph.

Fig. 39. The old Monkey Muck works.

Steel traps

Steel traps had been a staple trade for many, many years in Wednesfield. Both for home use, and for export, trapping anything from a mouse to a lion; yes, and even poachers!

Though their use here was made illegal some 200 years ago practically all production was by hand throughout from the iron and steel strip and bar, including forging the springs and so on. A big trade was done with Australia in rabbit traps. No doubt some traps made in Wednesfield were used in the wilds of North America, by the Hudson Bay company's trappers, to provide beaver, sable, and other valuable furs shipped to European countries. Whilst traps for lion, tiger, and leopard, had a ready market in Africa, India and the Far East.

Best known makers of traps were John Marshall, Lichfield Road, Henry Lane Ltd, Hickman Street, Joseph Collins, Graisley Lane, Samuel Marshall, Neachells Lane, Joseph Williams, Joseph Tonks, and there were others. W. Sidebotham were very well known for their trap making business in Rookery Street towards the rear of the New Inns. Mrs Nellie Foster born in March 1899, at the Orchard Buildings,

Fig. 40. Sidebothams steel trap works with the Monkey Muck in the background. The picture was taken in 1990.

Church Bridge, knew a thing or two about the old trap making days. She worked in the trade for a number of years; her husband Samuel Edwin Foster was a well known man about Wednesfield. He started a successful transport business in Hall Street in 1924, and was one of five founder members of the Road Haulage Association.

Japanned iron and steel trunks, and boxes were made by Messrs Pritchard & Sons, Hickman Street, who employed some fifty or so male and female works, for there was a big call for these types of goods at the time. About this time Mander Bros started up their paint works near Wednesfield Station.

Vaughn & Pedleys iron foundry, stood on the site of the Weldless Steel Tube works; the firm established their works in 1899.

A small tannery stood on the site of the present Lichfield Road school. Whilst on the corner of Taylor Street there was a small saddlers, where whips were plaited at marvellous speed, while round eyed youngsters looked on. Old Joe Turner had his blacksmiths and wheelwrights shop on the north side of the church.

T. Pallant & Sons with their fleet of motor lorries grew out of a small coal yard by Rookery Street Bridge. One horse and coal cart, and a covered carriers two wheeled cart, made weekly journeys with keys, and traps to Birmingham. The late Tom Griffiths also started with one horse and cart over 100 years ago, and developed the business of luxury motor coaches and lorries. A tiny place in Hickman Street was the origin of Thos. Squire & Co.

The ironmongers shop of Jabez Pritchard, Rookery Street, corner of Hall Street, later changed to Squires Hardware Store.

Richards and Ross

Richards and Ross was a small medium sized firm in Neachells Lane, they forged out a new identity, this is how it began, and nearly ended quickly.

The firm is now an independent company, over 58 years old. Over that period it has experienced many changes in fortune, most of the time as part of the international engineering group, Tube Investments.

The company business is carried on over a four and half acre site, most of which is covered; approximately 70 people were employed there.

The company was founded in 1931, by Penny Richards, and Charles Ross.

Both were previously at Weldless Steel Tube, now Seemless Tubes Ltd.

After the 1939-45 War, the Company's fortunes varied, but there were many prosperous years, however by the late 1970s, the problems of the country's manufacturing sector, and engineering, in particular, hit many firms in the West Midlands, including Richards and Ross.

Closures and redundancies became common, few firms escaped, like

Fig. 41. A view from the top of Rookery Street. The ground on the right staged fairs in c1900. The site was known as Johnny Carters' fields. The white building further down on the right was one of the four shops which stood next to Squires hardware shop, corner of Hall Street.

many companies Richards and Ross faced the problem head on, and forged out a new identity. In 1985 it became a private company again, following a management buy-out. This brief outline conceals a multitude of events, however, the company could have had a very limited life if the German Luftwaffe had been successful.

The company was thought sufficiently important to be a key target for one of the raids on the West Midlands in the early 1940s. Fortunately, the raid was not a success. Detailed documents showing the German plans to bomb the factory, came into the company's possession, about ten years later. Yes, the factory had a very close encounter.

10. Kids games and supersitions

Chickens and pigs

MANY people in Wednesfield kept poultry and livestock.

My family kept pigs for years when we lived in Tithe Road. My two brothers, Ron, Roy, and I, used to ride up and down the garden on our pigs, that was in the early 1950s.

We also kept chickens. I can remember my dad killing one every few weeks. He would first stun the fowl by hitting its head against the coal house door, and then he would nick its throat with a razor - the seven o' clock type if you can remember them - he would then hang it upside down and let the blood run out. It was then made ready for the oven. The feet would be cut off and we would play with them. The small piece of sinew that stuck out of the leg part would move if you pulled it.

I haven't seen this done for many years. I can remember a neighbour cut the head off a chicken, but it still ran round the garden.

Those days are long gone. Times were hard, but they still seemed good because you had to go without. That way, when you had something good you would appreciate it more. It would be fantastic to be able to step back in time whenever you wanted to meet loved ones. Will time travel ever become a reality? What a fantastic invention.

Wednesfield kids at play

Do you remember some of the things you used to get up to when you were a child? Here's a few games you may have played.

What about getting the grease proof paper from a loaf of bread, so that you could sit on it to make you go faster down the shute in Wednesfield Park.

Do you remember those balls of whitewash from Jimmy Lampoils in Wood End? Did you ever ride along the canal on one of the those coal barges? I did, it was great fun.

Did you ever go swimming in the cut? Were you brave enough to dive off the bridge? Remember those fishing rods, a stick with a bit of cotton tied on with a matchstick for a float, with a worm tied on the end.

What about those old fashioned gas lamps with the cross piece just under the lamp, we used to tie a rope to it and swing around.

Push bikes were all the rage in those days, you could see them in the mornings like a swarm of bees going to factories down Neachels lane, like Jenks and Cattell, and the Willenhall Radiator.

Gory Wednesfield

I wonder if you remember the horse that drowned under Church Bridge. It was pulling a barge and had its feed bag tied round its mouth, it slipped on the cobbles and fell in. It drowned because the men could not get its feed bag off quickly enough, they had to work hard to get the horse out of the cut.

Here's a name I don't want to know much about - Gerard Turner. Can you recall what he did for a living? He had the house that is now a dentists in Neachells lane. Pickerings did the same trade in Rookery Street, and no it was not a barbers. If you ever see the dentists, look at the windows, this is where, well..... I am not going to say anymore.

The legend of Helmsley Lodge

This story goes back to a time when superstitions cast much more awesome spells over the Black Country than they do today.

Terms which have been used to describe this house, Helmsley Lodge, have ranged from, an ill-fated house, to, it was built with blood money, to, it was built with other men's sweat.

Helmsley Lodge, in Wednesfield, was built reputedly with the proceeds of robberies from many country churches.

The villains of the piece, two Wednesfield brothers, ended their lives on the scaffold. But let's first tell the story. It has been going round the village quite some years.

The setting takes us back to the early 19th Century, when Wednesfield was a beautiful rural area where the old feudal order still remained, and the vast majority of its citizens were cast in a "Country Johnny" mould.

Amidst the scattered farmsteads, and labourers tied-cottages, "The

Pheasant" a rambling coaching inn typical of the era, was a place where local men used to "wet their whistles" and discuss the events of the day after long days in the fields.

The Pheasant was kept by the Mason family. It was a prosperous establishment, but two of the sons of the household were not content to wait for their inheritance and hit upon an ingenious scheme which brought them immediate cash dividends.

After flirting with "Highway Robbery" on nearby Watling Street, they found the game a trifle too risky, and devised a crafty plan which was extremely profitable yet involved little peril to their own necks.

Two of the family's string of horses kept in the stables at "The Pheasant" were selected and trained with the aid of the inn's ostler to return "home" unattended from various points "over the border" in Shropshire.

The two brothers would take them on their infamous missions to isolated churches in the Shropshire countryside, steal silver plate and any other items of value, load the booty into panniers and send them "trotting off" home whilst they returned on foot, by a different route. Their accomplice, ostler Bishop would be waiting in the stables at "The Pheasant" to receive the stolen goods and conceal them nearby until they could be "shared out" when the coast was clear.

The scheme worked perfectly until the brothers turned their attentions to country mansions in addition to churches. "The gentry" became alarmed at the countless unsolved burglaries taking place, and their influence led to Bow Street runners being posted to the area, with orders to 'apprehend' the culprits.

Some suspicion fell upon the Mason brothers for they showed signs of unaccountable wealth and built a large house 'Helmsley Lodge' close to their father's inn.

However, the Bow Street runners failed to 'twig' their crafty scheme and they might never have been caught but for the vigilance of the local blacksmith, whose smithy stood in Long Knowle Lane, en route for "The Pheasant", a petrol station was later built on the site, now five houses have recently been built there. The blacksmith was a light sleeper and on several occasions heard the loot ladened horses clattering by during the small hours.

He kept watch and saw that they were riderless and unattended. His curiosity was aroused and he made a point of following them, and saw the ostler taking the silver plate from the bulging panniers in "The Pheasant" stable yard and informed the Wednesfield constable of his discoveries.

The local lawmen sought the help of the Bow Street runners and the Mason brothers were kept under close watch from that moment onwards.

Needless to say they were eventually caught 'red handed' at the scene of their final crime, in the act of placing stolen goods in the panniers of their "homing horses".

Justice was swift in those days and a hangman's noose quickly ended their criminal activities.

The ostler in the case apparently escaped retribution sufficiently to tell the story to his grandson, Matt Bishop, who passed it on to a Mr Adams more than 90 years ago.

After the dual execution, Helmsley Lodge was sold and had many tenants during the following century, but it gained the reputation of being an ill-fated, and some said, haunted house.

Bad luck and ruin seemed to dog every succeeding tenant, and the house was eventually demolished to make way for housing developments. The old blacksmith's shop was demolished in 1952.

"The Pheasant" was rebuilt during the 1930s and the original building was built around 1640, a few hundred yards from the one standing today.

Vast changes have taken place in Wednesfield over the last hundred years, but many of the names of houses and people have continued to live on through time, like Helmsley Road, Wood End, close to where Helmsley Lodge used to stand.

One person I knew was Tony Holdcroft, he was born in Helmsley Lodge, he said that many strange occurrences took place in that house whilst he lived there, and that it was not all superstition.

One such occurrence heard were the sounds coming from the stairs, just like a horse stamping its feet, he also told me that he kept hedgehogs in a box under the stairs. One day they just vanished, mind you if I was his mother I would have put them outside, but he said this did not happen.

These were just two strange occurrences that took place whilst the Holdcrofts were tenants; there were more. People used to cross the road, rather than walk past the house; it was demolished between 1952 and 1953.

More supersitions

Another superstition perhaps remembered by our oldest inhabitants concerns Harts Road. At the bottom end towards the "tube", many strange things have been seen here over hundreds of years. It is said to have been a place where the devil, elves, and goblins have appeared. I must say that it does have an atmosphere about it, that I cannot explain.

As an extreme instance of superstition the occupier of a house in Frederick Road renumbered his premises 11A rather than keep 13; that was in 1960.

Strange-but-true tale by a Wednesfield man

Sometimes authors have their own story to tell. This is such an extraordinary tale I feel it must be documented. It is absolutely true. About ten years ago (1999), I worked as a driver for Parcel Force, delivering parcels on a daily basis. My route was, Wombourne, Trysull, Seisdon, and Claverley, very nice areas.

On the particular day in question, I had a delivery for No. 2 Chequers Avenue in Wombourne. This was basically the start of my round. I delivered a catalogue to that address. There was nothing strange about that. Then I completed the rest of Wombourne, moving on to Trysull. I then moved on to Seisdon, that's where the story really begins.

"I had to deliver to some stables in a road called Post Office Road. It was more like a country lane with houses dotted here and there. Anyway, I delivered to the stables which were down a dirt track just off this road. It was only a delivery of a bag of horse feed. I just left it by the stables there being no one around, then I drove back down the track. Upon getting back into Post Office Road I noticed a bedraggled dog walking along the road. Obviously it was lost by the state it appeared to be in. It was wet and windy, He looked very sorry for himself. Anyway, I stopped the van and got out to try to catch him. I could not. So I got my sandwiches from the van, corned beef. I shouted to him and whistled. He stopped and turned his head, he then walked towards me. I was gesturing with my sandwiches. Come on, come on, I won't hurt you! I heard myself telling him. He walked slowly towards me. He ate part of my sandwich as I patted him on the head. "There's a good boy..." I said to him. While he was eating one of my sandwiches I noticed a name tag on his collar, I gingerly put my hand on the tag, he growled a little but carried on eating the snack I had provided for him. Crikey! I could not believe it. His name was Benji, the address on the tag was No. 2 Chequers Avenue, Wombourne. What a coincidence. There was only one thing to do and that was to entice him into my van and return him to his owner, but how? The answer was quite simple. I opened the van door and threw a sandwich in. He fell for it immediately, and I shut the door.

"I decided to finish my round. Upon driving away Benji started barking quite loudly. I said to him if he could understand "I am taking you home."

He started to howl, though. So I drove along and I decided to stop at the post office in Seisdon to buy some chocolate for him.

"Continuing to Claverley, Benji still howled, even after he ate his Kit Kat. He began to annoy me. I told him again and again, I was taking him home. I thought dogs were clever. Why could he not understand. Anyway, I drove back to Wombourne. As we approached Chequers Avenue he seemed to quieten down. It had been about three hours since I rescued him. He must have recognised the area. "There you are... look at you, I have returned you home... I bet if you could talk you would thank me."

I pulled up outside the house. I told Benji to stay where he was whilst I knocked on the door. I knocked. Straight away I hear a dog bark. I thought to myself they must have two dogs. A woman appeared whom I had never seen before because I had only delivered a catalogue to her doorstep. I said feeling really proud of myself for returning her dog "Hello, I have found

Fig. 47. Wednesfield Church, in c1910. One of the houses to the right is where Mary Bodley once lived. To the left you can just see the chimney pots of the Boat Inn.

your dog...." The woman looked aghast. She said "What dog?... My dog is here, look." I remonstrated saying I had a dog in my van with her address on his tag. "Let me have a look at him" she said, upon that we went to the van and I opened the door. I grabbed Benji's collar. "Oh," she said, "that's not my dog, it's my daughter's, Benji." "But look," I said, "it's got your address on the collar tag." "Oh, my daughter must have forgotten to change the address. She moved about a month ago to... Post Office Road, Seisdon." "Whoops!" I said "that's where I found him.""

No wonder Benji howled he must have thought I was trying to kidnap him. I'll bet he was thinking you foolish human, how can I make you understand I live here. It just goes to show, dogs are not stupid animals, but humans can be.

11. Family, church and Christmas

I HAD many a belting off my dad. It never harmed me. In those days if you did wrong to anyone, or anything, you would expect a belting. If you aren't punished then what other deterrent is there to stop children misbehaving.

I must have held some sort of record for the number of canings at Neachells Lane School and March End. I don't hold any grudges against the teachers.

When I was a lad I knocked round with Barry Banks, Kenny and Tony Jordan, Frankie Hill, John Holdcroft, Albert and John Bickley. There were also my brothers Ron, and Roy. Ron was knocked over by a van on the main road outside Springhill Drapers in December 1967. He never recovered from his injuries and died on the 28th May 1968, aged 15. My father Ben died three years later. He never really got over Ron's death. My mother Muriel died in 1990. Many people know me, and my family, we have lived in Wednesfield most of our lives. One day I will go back to our old house in Tithe Road and have a look.

The thing about it all is you don't know until they've gone, how much you really loved them. We take so much for granted; they are there with you and then they are gone. It is the same the world over, but it never seems fair, because there is so much you need to do, to say to those you loved. God knows what he is doing, don't worry about that! They say he takes the best first. They have gone to a better place than what we live in today.

What do I believe

I don't go to church. It frightens me. But I believe there is an After Life; "I know there is...". Have you ever been doing something, at work, home, or school, and suddenly felt you have done this before, sometime, somewhere. Maybe in another time, or a parallel world; there is something, I know it. One day we will all meet up in another life, an-

Fig. 51. The houses on the left still stand today. They are now used as shops; one sells cards and things.

other time.

I believe above the storm the smallest prayer will still be heard. I believe that someone in the great somewhere hears every word.

Wednesfield's St Thomas' Church, 1751

Before 1747 Wednesfield was a common field, with a sparse population, and no place of worship nearer than Wolverhampton, Willenhall, and Bushbury. At that time an Act of Parliament (20. Geo. II. c. 27) was obtained "For building Wednesfield Chapel near Wolverhampton". A neat chapel of brick and stone was erected chiefly by the liberality of the members of the Gough family. This building being too small for the requirements of the increasing population was rebuilt, in 1842, and reopened on Shrove Tuesday February 28th 1843. The sum of £44 was collected at the opening service.

The first baptism was that of Mary, the daughter of John and Mary Webb, May 19th 1751.

Richard Shelden, the first person interred in the churchyard, was buried, April 13th 1751.

Fig. 48. All gathered round for the camera. Notice the three men at the back, two are wearing their flags.

Figures. 52 and 53. Wednesfield Wesleyan Chapel, corner of Alfred Squire Road. Built in 1886, it opened on Monday, July 19th 1886. The fence round the Chapel (see below) is no more. I wonder what happened to it?

On Sunday August 31st 1754, a smiling bride and bridegroom, the first married couple, were seen leaving the church. The happy pair were Joseph Curtis, widower, and Hannah Taylor, widow; a licence having been obtained, the work performed on that occasion, may have been an unexpected surprise to the quiet inhabitants of Wednesfield. Nearly one hundred years passed away until the second marriage took place. The first marriage, under the Registration Act, was that of John Leadbeater, and

Charlotte Hinton, on June 13th 1849. A casual glance at the church windows, on Saturday evening, January 18th 1902, lead to the discovery that the building was on fire. An alarm was raised, willing hands rang the bell for assistance, but too late, the flames had taken hold on the edifice. The organ, pulpit, every bench, gallery, pew, were consumed with fire. At length the belfry and roof were enveloped in flames. The communion table, choir stalls, surplice, cassocks, clothes for the table, two oak chancel chairs, and three stained-glass windows were saved.

The parish registers being kept in the Vicarage, and the communion plate in the vestry, were safely preserved.

At the time of the fire, it is reported that Wolverhampton Fire Brigade took half an hour to reach the site, having had to stop to rest their horses en route, and Willenhall Fire Brigade could not attend as no horses were available at the time.

The church was rebuilt using the outer walls and tower. It was reopened in 1903.

Since then little has changed with the exception of the wall round the building, now being about half the size it used to be. There are also fewer trees due to Dutch Elm disease, and there used to be a lamp above the door.

The exterior can hardly be described as beautiful, being built as it was originally in an age responsible for a great number of plain and even ugly buildings. The present interior is pleasing to the eye, and usually the churchman can worship in an atmosphere of warmth and comfort, which was not the case in the old days, but whether more devout and sincere is another matter.

I wonder what the people of 1751, who dedicated the original chapel to St Thomas the Apostle, would think of today's St Thomas Church, it being now some 260 years on since the original chapel building.

In the corner of the churchyard is a monument to the Bate family. John Bate was voluntary surveyor to Wednesfield vestry and local Government Board 1846-1949 and 1851. Amongst other things, he was responsible for ensuring that holes in the highway were filled in.

Christmas

"What is Christmas going to mean to you? Just a round of pleasure seeking and much over eating, or has life so embittered you that this Holy season leaves you cold and indifferent to its message of Peace and Goodwill; or will it mean that once again you re-dedicate your life to him, to whom Christmas owes its origin, and make room for him in your heart.

Are you rich, as far as this world's goods are concerned? Then share your good fortune with others

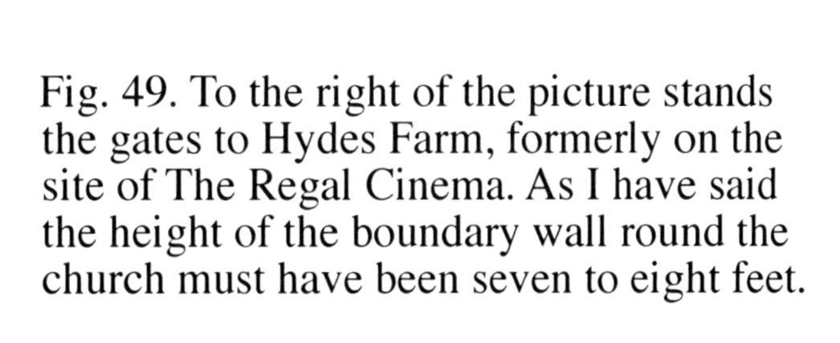

Fig. 49. To the right of the picture stands the gates to Hydes Farm, formerly on the site of The Regal Cinema. As I have said the height of the boundary wall round the church must have been seven to eight feet.

less fortunate, remember it is not what we have, but what we have given. Have you few of this world's goods? Then remember riches do not always bring happiness, so often they blind us to the true values, and things most worth having, money cannot buy, also remember God's son was born in a stable, and at times had nowhere to lay his head. God cares and loves you, altho' it may be hard to believe this fact at times.

Are you an invalid? Then remember it is far more important to be strong, in spirit, than bodily strength.

Have you a strong, healthy body? Then be thankful for it, and offer it back to God, to be used in his service.

Are there things in your life you know to be wrong? Then get down on your knees and humbly ask God's help. He is ever waiting to forgive, recreate, and refresh you by his Holy Spirit."

Fig. 50. Wednesfield Church, in the mid 1950s. Note the lovely old lamp post in the foreground. The photograph is taken from the bridge; it replaced the old one in 1922 .

This was a Christmas message from an edition of the *Wednesfield News*.

12. Staying at home, school, getting about, and home

The Old People's Welfare Centre

I remember the houses of Pickering Road being built just after 1958. I went to a wedding reception at the Old People's Welfare Centre. I'll bet Pickering Road was named after someone.

At the bottom end of the road, where the flats are, this used to be fields. One of them had a pond in. It was where we used to catch frogs and tadpoles.

The Old People's Welfare Centre was opened on September 8th 1956. Names of officers, and the Welfare Centre committee were:-

Chairman councillor S. Broomhall
Vice Chairman Mr J.R. Munslow
Treasurer Mr F.B. Smith

Many people helped this centre in those days and they all worked hard on the Flag and Envelope days. Many companies donated towards the upkeep of the Centre. Just a few I will mention were, the Wolverhampton Metal, The Willenhall Radiator, Griffiths Bros, A.E. Jenks and Cattell Ltd, W. Butler & Co., Mitchell and Butler, Atkinson brewery, Holt brewery, Fred Pickering (builders), Weldless Steel Tube, Richards and Ross, Squires Hardware, and Bolton Road Social Club, and there were many more.

The photograph shows the gathering of some of the elderly people of Wednesfield. Have a good look there's bound to be someone you can remember. My granny is on there. Her name was Florence Jones. She is to the left of centre next to Mrs Potts, she's the one in the cardigan.

Eva Tonks was the secretary of the Centre, and what a wonderful job she has done there.

The Cottage Homes

There were eight houses in the Cottage Homes and the cost was largely met by the ratepayers, unlike the voluntary organisations of the National Children's Homes, and Dr Bernardo's. Local donations however provided welcome extreme for the children, which was much appreciated. I have

Fig. 61. Could your mum or dad be on this photograph? Florence Jones and Mrs Potts are. They are in the middle of the photograph.

Mrs Potts is wearing the cardigan, with granny Jones to the left.

come across the date November 7th 1890 - was this its opening day?

The homes had a holiday camp in North Wales, the result of a bequest of £1,200 and many of the children used to go there for their summer holidays.

There were over 100 children with foster parents in the homes which meant that the superintendent and the children's officer had a very busy time.

There were two soccer pitches, and a cricket field, television was laid on and at one time the home possessed eight geese, several goats, and a donkey.

Cottage Homes, Wednesfield.

Children were sent to the Homes for various reasons, either through parental desertion, or ill-health, 25% were compulsory sent by the courts, or by arrangement between the parents and the local authority.

Each application was thoroughly investigated, and the policy of the Cottage Homes was to try to provide a normal life for the children. But in some cases, a child's place is in his own home.

Wednesfield schools

St Thomas' Church School was erected in 1856 for 299 mixed pupils. William Bentley Flats stand on the site. The wall round the school was some six feet high. It ran from the main gate, which would have been where Torridge Drive starts, up Graisley Lane, the other side of the playground, came up to the backs of the gardens in Hickman Street. Of course, the school across the road was erected some time later. But both schools were St Thomas' and they were both used, because of the increase in pupils.

Fig. 46. The Cottage Homes, Wednesfield.

Fig. 65. The Old Church School, at the turn of the last century, c1900.

Some teachers

For those who went to the Church School between 1950 and 1960, here is a list of some teachers who were there.

Mr Whelan, said by most to have been, a nice chap, and very much a favourite with the pupils; Maths and P.E. were his subjects.

Mr E. Ellis, nicknamed "Ecca", the headmaster.

Mr Lewis, nicknamed "Gong" because he made a black and white silent film about the school and on the title credits it said presented by Gong (I wonder where that film is now), took Geography for a short time.

Mrs Griffiths, nicknamed "Beak", an R.E. teacher.

Mr B Brough took science.

Miss Richards took English; Mr Brown taught Art, and Mr Hughes taught History. The woodwork master was Mr Davies and the music teacher was Mrs Onions. No doubt, there were many more. I hope you have happy memories of school days. I could not wait to leave, but after a couple of years I began to think School was not really so bad after all. It's just that you don't realise it at the time. It's the most important time of your life. School shapes your whole future, as to what work you seek, what qualifications you achieve, and also the friends you make.

Some dates of other schools in Wednesfield are as follows:

In 1837 a school was built in New Street. It was later used by a firm of coffin makers for a few years before being demolished in the early 1920s.

The Council, Lichfield Road, Infants was erected in 1911 for 400 pupils. Miss Lilian Marshall was headmistress in the early 1920s.

Long Knowle Juniors opened in January 1956.

Kitchen Lane opened in 1956, and part of Wards Bridge was opened in September 1956.

Wood End Church of England Infants opened on July 27th 1875 for 130 children; Miss Dorothy Price was headmistress in the early 1920s.

Wednesfield Grammar School received its first pupils on Wednesday, September 7th 1960. The school had already existed for one year, housed in temporary premises in Wednesbury.

The three storey building was for children who were successful in the 11 Plus examination, it started off with 450 pupils, but quickly rose to over one thousand with ages ranging from 11 to 18.

Neachells Lane School was built as a board school in 1895 for 507 mixed pupils, with the infants school erected in 1902.

Ashmore Park School opened in May 1959.

My schooldays

I started off my school days at Neachells Lane Infants. Dinner money was half a crown a week. I moved across to the Juniors and left at the age of eleven. Some of the teachers I can remember were Mr Wardle, headmaster, Mr Baxter, Maths and P.E., Ms Brotherhood (subject?), and a Polish teacher, who used to live in Graisley Lane opposite the Church School. I can't quite remember her name but Boy! could she throw a blackboard rubber, accurately.

I left Neachells Lane and went to Lichfield Road School because March End School was not ready. I was probably there for about six months before moving to March End, which was in January 1962.

The sports ground at the school had not yet been completed so we used the Church Field gardens. This field was fenced off from King George V's Playing Fields; some bungalows stand on the field now.

Fig. 64. Another St. Thomas School Inter Football team, Season 1938/9. The picture was taken in the old park. I wonder if any of these chaps served in the services in the Second World War.

Fig. 62. Church School Football team with Jack Morby

to the right of the photograph. 1947/8. Recognise anyone?

Fig. 63. Church School Inter Football team 1955/6. Mr Whelan
Bill Rushton, and one of the Howes' sons. Can you

to the right, Fred Snape, Dennis Harris,
name any more?

Trams and trolley buses

After the horse drawn trams came the single track electric trams running between Wolverhampton and Wednesfield, Broad Street to New Street route opened October 31st 1904. The route started at the top of Broad Street and finished at New Street. It took 10 to 12 minutes from town, having the only one track, there were about three loops. In order that the trams could pass, one of the loops was just outside New Cross main gates, another one was by the Star pub in Heath Town. If you can remember where that was, opposite the bank, corner of Cross and Railway Streets.

It was not unusual for the up going tram to have to wait 10 minutes for the down tram to pass.

The Wednesfield route had no overhead wires, the system was called the Lorain system, and the power came from a cable placed between the track lines and was obtainable from boxes placed at intervals.

From each box the tram could pick up enough power to keep it going. The track could not go over Rookery Bridge. Tram cars were taken off the Wednesfield route on 23rd July 1923. During the period of conversion a motor bus service was substituted. The first trolley vehicle ran from Broad Street to Wednesfield on 29th October 1923; the terminus in Wednesfield was at Pinfold Bridge, better known as Gregory's Bridge, an extension through the village beyond the former tram terminus. The vehicles were manufactured by Tilling-Stevens, they were single deckers with 40 seat centre entrance bodies. Six were purchased to operate this first service and numbers 1 to 6 were allocated, so that the numbers were duplicated on bus and trolly bus fleets.

These trolley buses were delivered in the new livery of apple green, and primrose.

For the first few years, the overhead wires were 12 inches apart, the more normal 18 inch space being used after 1930. For years Wednesfield had only single decker buses because of the railway bridge on the Wednesfield road. The problem was overcome eventually by lowering the roadway under it, but on one occasion a double decker bus took the wrong route and

Fig. 55. (Opposite bottom). The first electric trolley bus to run on the Wolverhampton to Wednesfield route, ran on October 29th 1923, and was Number 1 Reg DA 7741. It was a single decker with central side entrance. This photograph dates from c1923/4.

Fig. 56. A motor bus passing an electric trolley bus.

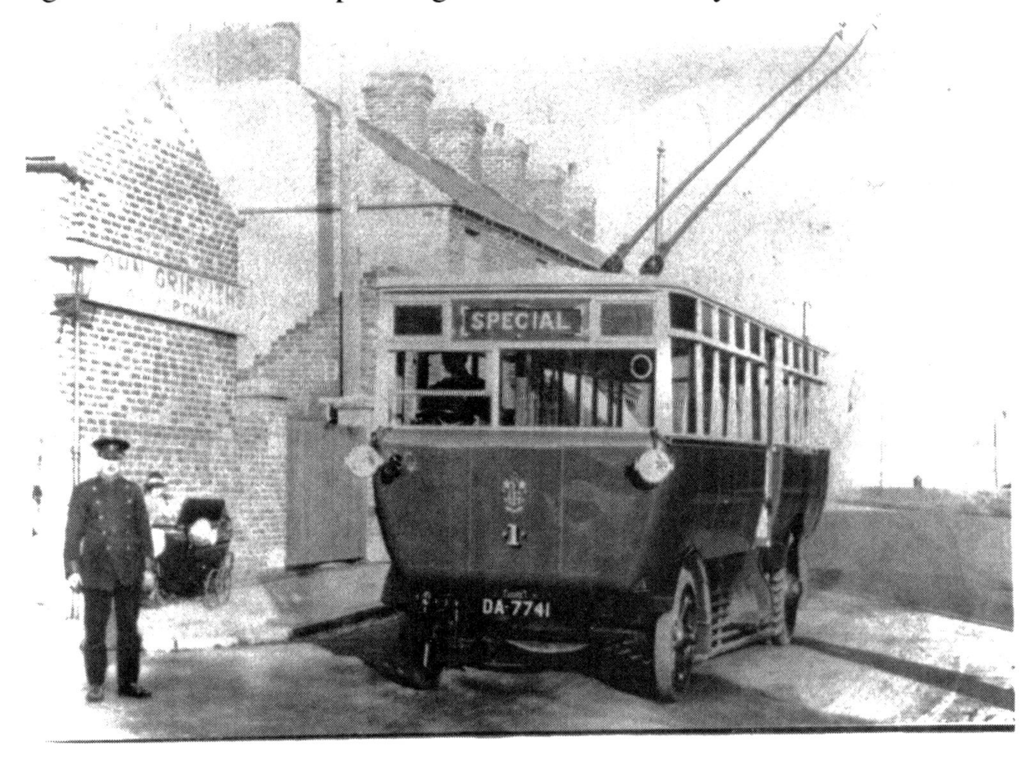

Fig.58. The Lorain track with the loop for trams to pass on the single track system. The view is looking towards Wednesfield at Heath Town.

Fig. 59. A Wednesfield tram on the road by Foulkes coal yard. This was as far as trams could go, in c1919/20.

Fig. 54. An early 1960s trolley bus on the High Street, Wednesfield. The Royal Oak Inn can be seen between the buses. The photograph also shows The Regal, a pet shop, Thompson's paper shop and the Wesleyan Chapel.

Fig. 60. The No. 59 on Broad Street Bridge. The Union pub is to the left. The Bridge went to the Black Country Museum.

got stuck under the bridge. No one knew how to get the bus out, and officials stood about scratching their heads and trying to come up with some ideas, until a schoolboy came up to them and said what about letting some air out of the tyres. They did this and were then able to pull the bus from under the bridge.

With the overhead power lines needed by the trolley buses it meant that they could at last go over the Rookery Bridge.

This still only went as far as the Dog and Partridge where they used to turn round, that was in the early 1920s.

Later on the trolley buses went as far as Wednesfield Island, and then later on to the Albion pub and then Ashmore Park.

One thing I remember about the trolley buses was how they used to come off the wires quite often, particularly at Wednesfield Island and the Rookery bend.

Tithe Road

Some back gardens of Tithe Road (the odd numbers) ran along the edge of the field known as Churchfield Gardens with the alley that runs from the Cross Guns to the playing fields on the other side.

The first block of houses in Tithe Road were demolished to make a road leading to the bungalows.

The numbers of those houses demolished to make way for an entrance road were: 1, 3, 5, 7, 9 and 11. The occupants at one time were Morris, Newey, Gommie Lovatt, Harris and Tommy Allen. I was born at Number 40 Tithe Road, next door to Buzzer Morgan, with Holdcrofts on the other side.

I lived there until the early 1970s. I now live in South Avenue, Nordley Hill; it's not too bad; there are worse places.

I hope you have enjoyed looking back at how Wednesfield used to be. One thing is for sure it will never be the same. But I hope you can relate to some of the things I have written about our village.

Authors in the future may write about Wednesfield, as they have in the past, but it's your own memories that really count.

Lightning Source UK Ltd.
Milton Keynes UK
02 August 2010

157659UK00002B/1/P